The Clinical Assessment
of Language Comprehension

The Clinical Assessment of Language Comprehension

by

Jon F. Miller, Ph.D.
Professor and Chair
Department of Communicative Disorders
Waisman Center on Mental Retardation and
  Human Development
University of Wisconsin–Madison

and

Rhea Paul, Ph.D.
Professor
Speech and Hearing Sciences
and
Director
Portland Language Development Project
Portland State University
Oregon

·P A U L·H·
BROOKES
PUBLISHING Cº

Baltimore • London • Toronto • Sydney

Paul H. Brookes Publishing Co.
Post Office Box 10624
Baltimore, Maryland 21285–0624

Typeset by Signature Typesetting & Design, Baltimore, Maryland.
Manufactured in the United States of America by
BookCrafters, Falls Church, Virginia.

Permission to adapt the following materials is gratefully acknowledged:
Pages 146–147, Procedure 4.2:   Paul, R. (1985). The emergence of pragmatic comprehension: A study of children's understanding of sentence-structure cues to given/new information. *Journal of Child Language, 12*(1), 167; adapted with the permission of Cambridge University Press.
Pages 151–155, Procedures 4.4–4.6:   Paul, R. (1995). *Language disorders from birth through adolescence: Assessment and intervention.* St. Louis: C.V. Mosby; adapted by permission.

Case studies described in this book come from composite multiple experiences of the authors. Names are pseudonyms. Any similarity to actual individuals or circumstances is coincidental and no implications should be inferred.

Readers have permission to photocopy the score sheets in this book for clinical purposes.

The plates on pages 66–113 were drawn by Dave Erickson.

Library of Congress Cataloging-in-Publication Data

Miller, Jon F.
   The clinical assessment of language comprehension / by Jon F. Miller and Rhea Paul.
      p.   cm.
   Includes bibliographical references and index.
   ISBN 1-55766-176-6
   1. Language disorders in children—Diagnosis.   2. Language acquisition—Testing.   I. Paul, Rhea   II. Title
   [DNLM: 1. Language Tests—in infancy & childhood.   2. Language Development   3. Cognition—in infancy & childhood.   WS 105.5C8 M648c 1995]
RJ496.L35M543   1995
618.92\855075—dc20
DNLM/DLC
for Library of Congress   94-35065
                                                                                                                                          CIP

British Library Cataloguing-in-Publication data are available from the British Library.

Contents

  • Developmental level: 8–24 months
  • Language level: Brown's stages I–II; MLU 1.0–2.5
  • Production milestones: At this level, children are producing single words and some early word combinations. Vocabulary size is generally small, fewer than 100 words. Few morphological markers are used. Phonological repertoire may also be limited, with certain consonants and syllable types (consonant-vowel-consonant [CVC], multisyllabic words) missing.

  • Developmental level: 24–60 months
  • Language level: Brown's stages III–IV; MLU 2.5–4.5
  • Production milestones: During this stage, children are acquiring the basic vocabulary and syntax of the language. Vocabulary size is expanding rapidly. Morphological markers are beginning to be used in speech. A variety of sentence forms, such as questions and negatives, are beginning to contain appropriate syntactic marking. Toward the end of the stage, complex sentences begin to be used. Phonological simplification processes may interfere with intelligibility.

4   Assessing Comprehension in the Language for Learning Stage . . . .
   • Developmental level: 5–10 years
   • Language level: Brown's stages V+; MLU 4.5 and up
   • Production milestones: Vocabulary is large (greater than 5,000 words). Basic
   syntax in simple sentences has been acquired; few grammatical errors are
   heard in speech. Some complex sentences (about 20% of utterances in speech
   samples from typically developing children [Paul, 1981]) are used. Most morphological markers are used consistently, although a few errors (e.g., overgeneralization of past tense) may persist. Most phonological simplification
   processes have been eliminated; one or two may remain. Distortions of a few
   sounds may also be present. Speech is intelligible.

About the Authors

Jon F. Miller, Ph.D., is Professor and Chair of the Department of Communicative Disorders and is Director of the Language Analysis Laboratory at the Waisman Center on Mental Retardation and Human Development Research Center, University of Wisconsin–Madison. Dr. Miller has published extensively in the areas of child language development and disorders, language assessment, and language intervention. His current research is focused on quantifying disordered language performance using computer-assisted language sample analysis software (SALT: Systematic Analysis of Language Transcripts) and a reference database of more than 250 typically developing children. In addition, he has been investigating early language development in children with Down syndrome in a longitudinal research project funded by the National Institutes of Health since 1988.

Rhea Paul, Ph.D., is Professor of Speech and Hearing Sciences at Portland State University, Director of the Portland Language Development Project, and a Fellow of the American Speech-Language-Hearing Association. She has published numerous research articles on children's language disorders and is author of *Pragmatic Activities for Language Intervention* and *Language Disorders from Birth Through Adolescence: Assessment and Intervention.*

Preface

This volume was written to provide clinicians and researchers with assessment tools for evaluating children who cannot meet the cognitive, perceptual, or motor requirements of standardized tests or to evaluate aspects of language not assessed by other published measures. The procedures presented here evolved from our clinical practice and the need to assess the language comprehension skills of children with a variety of developmental disabilities. We have always believed that assessing language comprehension in these populations is very important because comprehension status cannot be assumed from language production ability. In a variety of populations, with documented or suspected dysarthria or apraxia of speech, for example, it is essential to evaluate language comprehension to determine the extent to which productive language is limited by impairments of speech motor control, rather than limitations in language competence. As another example, research has shown that children with Down syndrome consistently show better language comprehension skills, relative to productive level. Although we do not understand the cause(s) of this gap, it is clear that these children's enhanced comprehension status must be documented in order to help parents understand their child's abilities and potential, to help teachers develop appropriate curricula, and to aid clinicians in focusing intervention strategies. As a final example, comprehension status is critical for evaluating children who are candidates for augmentative and alternative communication systems. If comprehension status can be documented, then appropriate language content can be developed for a communication device.

The diversity of the measures included in this volume reflects the complexity of language and the breadth of adaptations required to solve the clinical problems of assessing comprehension skills throughout the developmental period. The measures presented in this volume are not a comprehensive list of all possible informal methods of comprehension assessment. Instead they are intended to enhance our assessment repertoire, and their creative use will improve our ability to measure this private event, the understanding of language.

For the Reader

This book was written as a clinical manual for practicing speech-language pathologists. As such, it assumes a great deal of knowledge about children's language development and disorders. Readers who believe they need additional background information about the topics presented here may want to familiarize themselves with one of the many excellent textbooks on language development that are now available.

For readers using this book for the first time, it will help to read Chapter 1, and the introductory text to each of the second, third, and fourth chapters before trying any of the procedures. This material provides information about specific issues concerning language comprehension and its assessment. Reading Chapter 5 next will help put the whole enterprise in perspective. It demonstrates, with concrete examples, how the procedures given in the book can be used in the context of a comprehensive communication evaluation for children at a variety of developmental levels.

The procedures given in the book represent a sampling of the kinds of informal assessments that can be used to enhance our understanding of the comprehension skills of very young or hard-to-test children. We do not intend that every procedure be used with every child a clinician sees. Rather, the procedures given here are meant to supplement more standardized forms of assessment, and to augment the picture of a child's comprehension skills. As the examples in Chapter 5 show, often only one or two procedures will be selected for each assessment case. These procedures will be used in conjunction with a range of tests, language sample analyses, and behavioral observations, in order to obtain a broad portrait of a child's communicative competence. Clinicians should, of course, select procedures that are appropriate for the developmental level of the child, using the production milestones guide given in each chapter. Selection of procedures will also be dictated by questions left unanswered by other aspects of the assessment. For example, if a clinician finds that a child fails to answer *where* questions on a standardized comprehension test, using a nonstandardized procedure to explore question comprehension can help determine whether the child does better in a friendlier, richer environment and, if so, whether the child can use cues in the discourse to help improve performance. If he or she can, the findings of the standardized test results can be balanced against our understanding of the situations in which the child can succeed.

Clinicians should also bear in mind that the procedures given here are merely examples. Our hope is to get clinicians thinking about comprehension, so they can develop their own informal methods of investigating this important aspect of communication. None of these procedures is meant as the "last word"; rather each is intended as a beginning, a way to initiate a larger set of methods to be used and shared clinically. Clinicians are encouraged to take off from these procedures and create new ones that address other areas, other developmental levels, or other kinds of disabling conditions.

Sample score sheets are provided at the end of Chapters 2, 3, and 4. They are marked with black tabs for easy reference, and readers are granted permission to photocopy them as needed. They are, however, just examples. Clinicians can create any form that they find efficient to use. We encourage clinicians to experiment with modifying the score sheets given here in order to find the most effective way of recording clinical data. Similarly, many of the score sheets include linguistic stimuli (words or sentences) that can be used as assessment items. These, too, are only examples. Clinicians may use them, if they are appropriate for a particular child; however, they do not have to be used. Any linguistic stimuli that address the issue being assessed are acceptable. The important points to ensure are that the child knows the individual words in the procedure before testing any comprehension of multiword sentences, and that the stimuli are appropriate for the interests and abilities of the child. If the examples on the score sheet don't meet these criteria, clinicians should not use them. Instead, they should create others that address the needs of the child. The strength of informal assessment is its flexibility. We strongly encourage readers to take advantage of that flexibility, using this manual as a guide, rather than as gospel.

Acknowledgments

We thank master clinicians Peggy Rosin and Gary Gill for their clinical insight, expertise, and enthusiasm, which sparked the creation of many of the procedures presented in this volume. Certainly their work with student clinicians evaluating children with a variety of developmental disabilities played an important role in the evolution of these measures to their present form. We also thank our colleague Robin Chapman for her many contributions to our understanding of children's development in general and of comprehension skills and strategies in particular, and her wise counsel on so many things.

Generations of students have passed through the Language Assessment Seminar and the Waisman Center Developmental Disabilities Clinic, creating and testing new comprehension procedures to meet their clients' needs. Their contributions to this work are gratefully acknowledged.

We also recognize Leslie Miller, John Chapman, Gary Gill, and Peggy Rosin, who served as models for the drawings used in Procedure 3.7.

Finally, we are indebted to Kathy Boyd, our editor, for her brilliant solution to the format problem this book presented, and the staff at Brookes Publishing Co. for their creativity and enthusiasm for this book.

To our children:

Karen, Leslie, and Meghan

Willy, Marty, and Aviva

The Clinical Assessment
of Language Comprehension

1 ◇ Understanding Comprehension and Comprehension Assessment

Since the early 1970s, during the explosion of knowledge in the field of child language and language pathology, we have learned a tremendous amount about the process of linguistic development. One thing we have learned is that language comprehension and production, while following predictable patterns of acquisition in most children, do not always correspond perfectly to each other, even in an individual child. Paul (1990), for example, discussed research showing that children who can produce certain syntactic forms, such as sentences with appropriate subject-verb-object word order, often are unable to demonstrate comprehension of the same sentences in formal testing situations. It seems that the traditional wisdom that "comprehension precedes production" is not operating—at least for some structures and during some developmental periods. To us, as clinicians, this is more than an interesting empirical finding. It means that we cannot make assumptions about language comprehension on the basis of a child's production, or vice versa. It also means that in order to get a complete picture of a child's language competence, each modality of language will have to be assessed independently.

In this book, we present a series of informal, nonstandardized procedures and activities that can be used to assess children's understanding of spoken language. Beginning in 1980, these procedures have been developed in the diagnostic evaluation clinic at the Waisman Center, an interdisciplinary training and research center at the University of Wisconsin–Madison, which serves a population of young children with developmental disabilities and multiple disabling conditions, by a variety of student and professional clinicians. The procedures were developed in response to the need to get a detailed picture of the receptive language ability of difficult-to-test children with a variety of disabilities at a range of developmental levels. The procedures are norm referenced in the sense that they were constructed with normal developmental data on comprehension acquisition in mind. A brief overview of the typical sequence of comprehension skills acquisition is presented in Table 1.1, along with some of the strategies typically used at each level. Clinicians can relate the comprehension performance they observe both to typical acquisition and to the child's level of language production, cognition, and other areas assessed in response to the procedures in this book. This information can help to develop a profile of performance, like the one shown in Figure 1.1. This profile can be used to describe a child's baseline level of language and cognitive skills, to determine intervention priorities, and to serve as a benchmark for progress in the intervention program. Miller (1981) described the use of such developmental profiles in detail.

It is important to bear in mind, however, that although the procedures presented here are norm referenced, they are not standardized.

Table 1.1.   Summary of comprehension development and strategies in children

Approximate age range	Normal comprehension skills	Possible strategies
8–12 months: Comprehension of routines	Understands a few words in context (e.g., plays peekaboo when mom says words and models gestures, responds to direction "splash" if in tub)	1. Look at objects that mother looks at. 2. Act on objects at hand. 3. Imitate ongoing action.
12–18 months: Lexical guides to context-determined responses	Understands single words for objects in immediate environment Will get an object if told to when object is in view Will perform some actions (e.g., kiss, hug, pat) with verbal instruction alone Knows names of familiar people Average receptive vocabulary size: 12 months: 3 words 15 months: 50 words 18 months: 100–150 words	1. Attend to objects mentioned. 2. Take objects offered. 3. Do what you usually do with objects at hand: a. Objects into containers b. Conventional use
18–24 months: Lexical comprehension but context determines sentence meaning	Understands two-word combinations similar to those produced including: action-object agent-action possessor-possession entity-location action-location Understands words for objects that are out of view Does not process three-term relations (e.g., agent-action-object) fully Average receptive vocabulary size: 150–500 words	1. Locate the objects mentioned and give evidence of notice. 2. Do what you usually do with objects at hand: a. Objects into containers b. Conventional use 3. Act on objects in way mentioned: a. Child-as-agent b. Choose handier object as instrument
24–42 months: Context-influenced comprehension	Understands three-term relations (agent-action-object) but has difficulty using word order to identify agent versus object in improbable (e.g., Baby feeds mother) or neutral (e.g., Horse pushes cow) sentences Understands who, what, where, and whose questions Average receptive vocabulary size: 300–1,000 words	1. Do what is usually done: a. Probable location strategy for in, on, under, and beside b. Probable event strategy for simple active reversible sentences 2. Supply missing information (2 years) to questions not understood. 3. Supply explanation (3 years) to questions not understood. 4. Infer most probable speech act in context.
42–48 months: Emerging syntactic comprehension	Understands word-order cues to agent-action-object relations Understands how questions Average receptive vocabulary size: 1,000–3,000 words	Comprehension of word-order cues to agent-object in active sentences (word-order strategy) when probability does not distract Word-order strategy overgeneralized to passive
4–8 years	Understands syntactic cues in basic sentence forms	Order of mention of clauses Probable relation of events strategy for causal conjunctions

(continued)

Table 1.1.   *(continued)*

Approximate age range	Normal comprehension skills	Possible strategies
4–8 years *(continued)*	Begins to learn exceptions to basic rules (e.g., passive sentences) Understands *when* questions Average receptive vocabulary size: 3,000–8,000 words	Understanding of contrastive conjunctions *but* and *although* as though they mean *and then* when probable relation not obvious

Adapted by permission from Chapman, R. (1978). Comprehension strategies in children. In J.F. Kavanaugh & W. Strange (Eds.), *Language and speech in the laboratory, school, and clinic* (pp. 309–327). Cambridge, MA: MIT Press.

This distinction means that the procedures have not undergone the extensive psychometric studies necessary to determine their reliability, validity, standard error of measurement, and so forth. The advantage of their lack of standardization is that they can be adapted in any way to any child's needs and abilities, unlike standardized tests, which must be given precisely according to the manual's instructions to preserve their psychometric properties. Because they are not standardized, these procedures cannot be used to determine *if* a child's comprehension skills are significantly different from those of typically developing children. To make that determination, a standardized instrument must be used. However, if a child has performed below criterion on standardized testing, or has already been diagnosed as demonstrating a significant language disorder, the procedures in this book can be used to compare comprehension to production skills, to investigate a range of different receptive abilities, and to help set priorities among intervention goals.

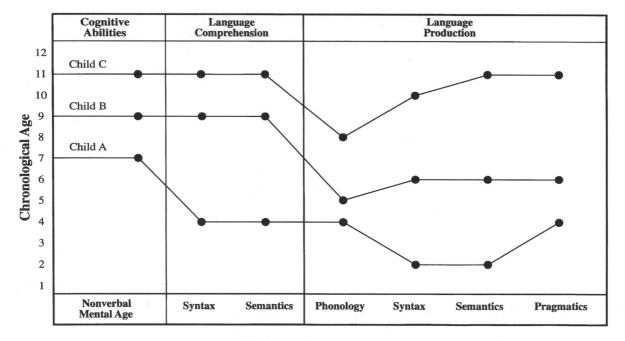

Figure 1.1.   Developmental profiles of three children. Child A has language comprehension and production delayed relative to nonverbal cognitive abilities. Child B has language production delayed relative to language comprehension and nonverbal cognitive abilities. Child C's language is developing normally, with language production and comprehension equal to nonverbal cognitive status and chronological age. Only phonological production is delayed. (From Paul, R. [1995]. *Child language disorders from birth through adolescence: Assessment and intervention*. St. Louis, MO: C.V. Mosby; reprinted by permission.).

The procedures are presented in developmental order, from those appropriate for children whose language is just beginning to emerge through those aimed at assessing language necessary for success in school. The procedures are divided into chapters based on three developmental levels, using the terminology employed by Paul (1995). The developmental level refers to the *linguistic* stage, based on production performance, in which a child is currently functioning, rather than to the child's chronological age. To do an informal assessment of comprehension, you would need to identify a child's level of linguistic production, either through language sample analysis (Miller, 1981; Miller & Leadholm, 1992) based on the child's mean length of utterance (MLU) and corresponding language level in Brown's stages (see Table 1.2), or more informally by simply having a short conversation with the child and selecting a general production stage by recognizing the production milestones listed below. Suppose, for example, you are seeing a 6-year-old child with Down syndrome. During a short chat around a set of toys, you might observe that the child produces primarily one- and two-word sentences. After confirming with the parent or caregiver that this production is typical for the child, you would assess comprehension by starting at the language level that corresponds to this linguistic performance: the emerging language stage. If the child performs well on the comprehension assessments for this stage, you can go on to testing higher levels. Testing would continue until a ceiling level of performance, indicated by an inability to respond correctly to a majority of items probed, is reached. Many children with limited production skills have more advanced receptive abilities, but current production level provides a logical place to start comprehension evaluation. The chapters in this book, then, are organized as follows:

Table 1.2.　Predicted MLU ranges and linguistic stages of children within one predicted standard deviation of predicted mean

Age ± 1 mo.	Predicted MLU[a]	Predicted SD[b]	Predicted MLU ± 1SD (middle 68%)	Brown's stages within 1 SD of predicted MLU							
				EI	LI	II	III	EIV	LIV/EV	LV	Post V
18	1.31	.325	.99–1.64	X	X						
21	1.62	.386	1.23–2.01	X	X	X					
24	1.92	.448	1.47–2.37	X	X	X					
27	2.23	.510	1.72–2.74		X	X	X				
30	2.54	.571	1.97–3.11		X	X	X	X			
33	2.85	.633	2.22–3.48			X	X	X			
36	3.16	.694	2.47–3.85			X	X	X	X		
39	3.47	.756	2.71–4.23				X	X	X	X	
42	3.78	.817	2.96–4.60				X	X	X	X	X
45	4.09	.879	3.21–4.97					X	X	X	X
48	4.40	.940	3.46–5.34					X	X	X	X
51	4.71	1.002	3.71–5.71						X	X	X
54	5.02	1.064	3.96–6.08						X	X	X
57	5.32	1.125	4.20–6.45							X	X
60	5.63	1.187	4.44–6.82							X	X

From Miller, J., & Chapman, R. (1981). The relation between age and mean length of utterance in morphemes. *Journal of Speech and Hearing Research, 24,* 154–161; reprinted by permission.

[a]MLU is predicted from the equation MLU = −.548 + .103 (AGE).

[b]SD is predicted from the equation SD MLU = −.0446 + .0205 (AGE).

Chapter 2: Assessing Comprehension in the Emerging Language Stage

- Developmental level: 8–24 months
- Language level: Brown's stages I–II; MLU 1.0–2.5
- Production milestones: At this level, children are producing single words and some early word combinations. Vocabulary size is generally small, fewer than 100 words. Few morphological markers are used. Phonological repertoire may also be limited, with certain consonants and syllable types (consonant-vowel-consonant [CVC], multisyllabic words) missing.

Chapter 3: Assessing Comprehension in the Developing Language Stage

- Developmental level: 24–60 months
- Language level: Brown's stages III–V; MLU 2.5–4.5
- Production milestones: During this stage, children are acquiring the basic vocabulary and syntax of the language. Vocabulary size is expanding rapidly. Morphological markers are beginning to be used in speech. A variety of sentence forms, such as questions and negatives, are beginning to contain appropriate syntactic marking. Toward the end of the stage, complex sentences begin to be used. Phonological simplification processes may interfere with intelligibility.

Chapter 4: Assessing Comprehension in the Language for Learning Stage

- Developmental level: 5–10 years
- Language level: Brown's stages V+; MLU 4.5 and up
- Production milestones: Vocabulary is large (greater than 5,000 words). Basic syntax in simple sentences has been acquired; few grammatical errors are heard in speech. Some complex sentences (about 20% of utterances in speech samples from typically developing children [Paul, 1981]) are used. Most morphological markers are used consistently, although a few errors (e.g., overgeneralization of past tense) may persist. Most phonological simplification processes have been eliminated; one or two may remain. Distortions of a few sounds may also be present. Speech is intelligible.

Before describing in detail the procedures for assessing comprehension, it is important to discuss the process of comprehension: what it means, why it is important, why it may present some unique assessment difficulties, and how we can address these difficulties in the evaluation process.

WHAT IS COMPREHENSION?

Comprehension, understanding, listening, and *receptive language* are terms we all use so frequently in the practice of speech-language pathology that we rarely stop to ask ourselves what we mean by them. In the most general sense, *linguistic comprehension* refers to the ability to interpret and make sense of spoken or written language. This includes the ability to associate words with the objects and the events they represent in a particular language (i.e., lexical knowledge) and the ability to decode the relationships among words encoded by particular grammatical devices and to understand the ideas conveyed by sentences (i.e., semantic/ syntactic knowledge). Of course, comprehension of language requires much more than linguistic comprehension. If it didn't, computers would comprehend everyday speech and translate one language into another with ease. The reason that we do not have such computers is that a great deal of additional knowledge that has little to do with words and sentences is needed to make sense of everyday conversation. Here are just a few examples of this additional knowledge:

1. *Social knowledge* and understanding of *intentionality* tell a child that when Mom says, "Do you want to be sent to your room without supper?", she is not asking a question to obtain information about preferences and requiring a yes-or-no answer. Instead she is issuing a threat to be responded to by ending the trampoline game on the sofa.

2. Understanding the *preparatory* and *sincerity conditions for speech acts* allows us to interpret the response "Is the Pope Catholic?" to our query "Are you hungry?" as a "yes" answer. We can do this because we know that it would be insincere to ask a question to which it was obvious that both the speaker and the listener already know the answer. We figure, then, that the question was not meant literally, but was used in order to convey something else. Probably, the speaker meant that the answer to our question is as obvious as the answer to his or hers.

3. Understanding of *cohesive devices,* which are linguistic markers that tell us that we need to look beyond an individual sentence to other parts of a text in order to grasp the full meaning of a passage. When we read "Alice ate the cake," for example, we realize that the speaker is referring to a previously mentioned pastry. We know we need to search our working memory for some prior reference to a cake in the text.

4. *Scriptal knowledge* tells us that when the cashier at the fast food counter says, "What'll it be?", our answer should consist of something on the posted menu, and not "Sunny tomorrow."

5. Knowledge of the *presuppositions,* or underlying assumptions, inherent in certain words allows us to understand that when a friend tells us some neighbors "*managed* to sell their house," we can divine not only that the house was sold, but that the real estate market is not at its peak in that neighborhood.

6. Other kinds of presuppositions are derived from *knowledge about the world,* rather than from words and sentences themselves. A worried politician might, for example, say ominously to her aide, "It's raining." The aide must understand the candidate's presupposition that rain means fewer voters will go to the polls and fewer voters at the polls mean fewer votes for the candidate.

7. *Specific background knowledge* ensures that, when our softball teammate says, "You're no Sandy Koufax," we resolve to volunteer for the outfield rather than asking to pitch in the next game.

8. *Inferencing* is involved in comprehension of sentences such as, "I got hungry while I was shopping, so I got a burger." Here the listener

infers that the burger did not appear out of midair, but that the speaker went to a restaurant and ordered a hamburger, which was served and for which he or she paid. Speakers know they do not need to include all of this information in their utterances, but can rely on listeners to make reasonable inferences based on knowledge of how things ordinarily happen in the world.

In other words, working out the literal meaning of what we read or hear—identifying the referents of single words and decoding the meaning relations within sentences—is just one part of the comprehension process. Let's call it the *literal level* of comprehension, for want of a better term. Other aspects of comprehension involve making judgments based on social, textual, scriptal, and other forms of prior knowledge to figure out what an utterance *really* means, in relation to what else has gone on in the discourse and to the intentional state of the speaker. We will refer to this as the *discourse level* of comprehension. Both literal and discourse levels are crucial to a listener's ability to get the full range of meaning from language.

PROBLEMS IN ASSESSING COMPREHENSION

Talking, like comprehending, of course, involves the coordination of a multitude of skills and spheres of knowledge. Although it is not always possible to know all of the processes that occur before the production of an utterance, at least we have the talk itself to analyze when we attempt to characterize a child's language production skills. But what do we examine when we assess comprehension? Comprehension is an event that takes place privately within the mind of the listener. It is often possible to judge whether listeners have understood us by means of their response in either words or actions. However, it is easy to think of situations in which apparently appropriate responses are used to give us the impression of comprehension when, in fact, none has occurred. Many of us might use tactics such as head-nodding, "um hm-ing," or adopting an intense facial expression, for example, to give a professor the idea that we have understood a lecture that, in fact, went completely over our heads. We might use the same tactics to appear to be following a description of the joys of step aerobics at a party at which we were really more intent on overhearing the name of the new arrival in tight jeans. Similarly, it is quite simple to imagine a situation in which comprehension has taken place but no overt evidence of it is given. Again, the lecture situation is a good example. A student can easily listen to a lecture, understand its content, and not give any outward sign of understanding until, perhaps, the day of the final exam.

Because comprehension differs from speech in that it is basically a private event, certain problems arise when we think about assessing a child's comprehension abilities. It seems obvious that the most valid way to assess a child's language production is to listen to what he or she says in spontaneous speech, tape record it, write it down, analyze it in some systematic way, and compare the result to developmental norms (Miller, 1981). Unfortunately, deciding on the most valid method for assessing comprehension is more problematic. The previous discussion described how adults use certain strategies, such as looking intently at the speaker and nodding the head, in order to appear to be listening or understanding when they really may not be doing either. Children also adopt some tactics for appearing to process linguistic input when they are, in fact, relying on the nonlinguistic context or a small portion of the linguistic signal in choosing a response. These strategies are discussed later in this chapter. For now, we need to be aware that they must be taken into account in the assessment process.

This problem brings us to the second difficulty in assessing comprehension: the need to examine both the literal and discourse levels of comprehension. Assessment with standardized tests has generally concentrated exclusively on the lexical and semantic/syntactic levels. The most widely used comprehension tests focus on vocabulary, morphology, and syntax. These tests have been criticized for failing to evaluate the complete range of operations the listener performs in understanding utterances in even the most common communication situations (Rees & Shulman, 1978). As we have seen, decoding the literal meaning of isolated sentences, like the ones usually used in formal comprehension testing, is only one piece of the comprehension process. To assess comprehension of literal meaning alone leaves open several other questions about the real process of understanding. For example, does the child understand the speaker's intention, the illocutionary force of the utterance? That is, can the child decide that "Can you pass the salt?" requires an action, rather than a yes-or-no answer? Can the child use information outside the sentence to determine how old information in the discourse relates to the new information being conveyed? Can he or she make appropriate inferences from the information given?

An additional problem with the assessing of discourse-level comprehension skills is that it is difficult to know what aspect of the signal the child is responding to, especially if traditional methods such as formal tests that remove extralinguistic cues are not used. When the child "demonstrates comprehension" by following an instruction in a natural setting, we do not know whether the child is responding correctly to the words, the context, prior knowledge, or some combination of cues. If, alternatively, the child fails to respond appropriately, at what level of processing has this failure occurred? In conversation, failures to derive the speaker's meaning may occur at one or more levels, including the interpretation of intent, the decoding of grammatical structure, or the understanding of single words. In order to interpret failures at discourse levels of processing, we will want to ensure that more basic lexical/syntactic aspects of comprehension have proceeded successfully. For example, a visiting 4-year-old child may not reply properly when asked, "When are you supposed to go home?" for either of two reasons. The word *when* may require knowledge of time concepts beyond her current level of lexical/cognitive development, or she may have failed to interpret the speech act as a polite suggestion that it is time to leave. A child with a language disorder who has relatively good pragmatic, or discourse-level, comprehension and can guess at a speaker's general intentions even though he or she has little knowledge of the propositional content of an utterance, may be generally better off than a child with poor literal and discourse-level skills. Nevertheless, both children will still be severely limited in the ability to gain meaning from interaction.

These three problems—the private nature of comprehension, the need to assess both literal and discourse-level abilities, and the difficulty in contextualized situations of knowing what levels of comprehension skills are operating or breaking down—are the ones that must be solved in order to get a complete picture of a child's comprehension skills. Before we try to solve these problems, though, let's ask a more basic question.

WHY ASSESS COMPREHENSION?

Why is it important to know about a child's abilities with both the literal and discourse levels of comprehension? Isn't it enough to assess language production and develop intervention goals based on those results? Lahey (1988) concluded from her review of research on comprehension versus production training that comprehension responses, such as pointing to contrastive stimuli, do *not* need to be trained before production of the forms is targeted. Guided production activities appear to facilitate both comprehension and production of the new forms in children. So, why worry about a child's comprehension skills? There are several reasons clinicians should be encouraged to assess comprehension skills in their clients.

To Ensure Eligibility for Services

There are basically two kinds of language disorders in children: disorders of only production, and disorders of both comprehension and production (Miller, 1987a; Miller, Campbell, Chapman, & Weismer, 1984). Disorders of only production are more common than disorders involving both modalities (Bishop & Edmondson, 1987; Miller, Chapman, Branston, & Reichle, 1980), but both types of disorders do exist, and there are reasons that we need to be able to distinguish between them. One reason has to do with eligibility for services and the type and intensity of intervention a child will receive. Children with documented impairments in two areas, such as language production and comprehension, can often qualify for more frequent or earlier intervention than children with disorders in only production.

To Help in Selection of Intervention Modality

Another reason to assess comprehension concerns the choice of a modality for intervention. In cases of severe production limitations, such as speech motor abnormalities associated with conditions like cerebral palsy, knowing a child's comprehension status can determine whether or not an augmentative and alternative modality, such as sign language or a communication board, should be introduced. Children with severe speech motor limitations but more advanced comprehension abilities have more to gain from an alternative system because they have a solid receptive foundation on which to build a production system. Those with little speech and limited comprehension abilities will benefit less rapidly from an augmentative system because they have less receptive groundwork on which a production repertoire can be based (see Paul [1995] for more detailed discussion of this issue).

To Select Appropriate Intervention Goals and Activities

As Fey (1986) points out, forms a child comprehends but does not produce are high-priority intervention targets, because the comprehension performance indicates the forms are, in Vygotsky's (1962) terms, in the child's "zone of proximal development" (ZPD), which refers to tasks the child is able to do with help and scaffolding from an adult, but cannot yet do alone. For example, adults often teach children to write their names by drawing dots to guide the child's first attempts:

Using this scaffolding, the child achieves something he or she could not yet do alone. Activities within a child's ZPD are within the reach of learning.

Alternatively, if a form is neither comprehended nor produced, some additional exposure, in the form of enriched input language during child-centered play sessions or focused stimulation activities (Fey, 1986), may be an especially important component of the intervention program. So, we would like to know whether or not a child can understand forms he or she does not say. This knowledge will determine the goals and activities that get high priority in the intervention program.

To Compare Comprehension in Contextualized and Decontextualized Settings

It is also important to know about a child's comprehension skills because very often they appear to be better than they are. The reason for this has to do with our two levels of comprehension. Although it might seem logical that children would learn literal comprehension before discourse-level skills, in fact the opposite is, to some extent, true. Children very often learn to take advantage of information present in social situations to help them respond to speech directed to them, essentially shortcutting literal comprehension and relying primarily on some aspects of discourse-level knowledge. These shortcuts, or *comprehension strategies* (Chapman, 1978), are used at early ages to allow children to make a guess at a speaker's intentions before they can actually process the lexical and syntactic information in sentences. Table 1.1 presents a summary of these comprehension strategies used at various developmental levels.

Of course, these comprehension strategies will only work in a very friendly atmosphere where everything is arranged to ensure the child's success. In order for the child to be successful, parents or caregivers must choose utterances judiciously, based on knowing what the child is likely to do, and conversation must be focused on objects and events immediately perceivable by the child. We can refer to this friendly situation as a *contextualized comprehension* setting. The context provides a great deal of information that is helpful in figuring out what people are talking about. However, many comprehension situations are *decontextualized*. They contain few cues beyond the words and sentences themselves that help a listener derive meaning. Talking on the telephone is one example of decontextualized conversation. The kind of language used in school, which often refers to events that are removed from the immediate context in space and time, is another. In order to operate in the wider world, children will eventually need to learn more reliable linguistic rules for extracting propositional meaning and to combine this meaning with other knowledge in order to arrive at complete understanding. They will need, in other words, to function not only in contextualized listening situations, but also in decontextualized ones. When we assess comprehension in children, we will want to know about the ability to make sense of language in both contextualized and decontextualized situations.

Examining use of comprehension strategies is one way to examine these two levels. We can set up both friendly, contextualized tasks, and more decontextualized situations for probing the same form. When children with language production problems do in fact understand, in both the contextualized and decontextualized format, more words and sentences than they say, less emphasis on exposure to target forms and more focused elicitation of targets can be the focus in the intervention program. Some children may perform well in the contextualized setting by employing a comprehension strategy. But, they may fail the same item in the decontextualized test. These children, who are showing good discourse-level comprehension but less accurate literal comprehension, may need additional exposure in intervention to gradually less contextualized settings in which consistent language forms are presented. Children who perform poorly in both contextualized and decontextualized settings, who do not take advantage of social and situational context to take a stab at a speaker's meaning, may have a more severe or pervasive disorder (Paul, 1990). Children like these may require more intensive intervention that addresses both language and, more broadly, cognitive-social issues.

WHY USE INFORMAL ASSESSMENT?

There are some well-constructed, psychometrically sound tests that are commercially available for assessing language comprehension. Table 1.3 provides a sampling of procedures developed for a range of language levels. When we assess comprehension with formal, standardized tests, we are assessing the first level of comprehension described in this chapter: recognizing the referents for words and the literal meaning of sentences. This level of comprehension is, of course, crucial to understanding language. Therefore, part of the comprehension assessment process will be to determine whether this aspect of listening is causing a child problems. For many children, standardized tests will be the most efficient, effective way to make this determination. So, what is the role of informal comprehension procedures? Let's look at some of the reasons informal assessment of comprehension is an important part of the language evaluation.

To Assess Areas Important for a Specific Child

First, standardized tests are designed to answer a specific question: Is this child different from other children? Often, we already know the answer to that question. What we really want to know is whether this child understands a particular word, structure, or discourse function. To answer this question, we will generally need more than one or two instances of performance on the target form or function to make a determination. Nonstandardized procedures provide an opportunity to test a form or function several times, in several contexts, or to use item-level analysis to pinpoint the child's problem area(s) that may require intervention. Standardized tests are designed to sample a small number of structures that are efficient in differentiating children at differing developmental levels. But often we want to know whether a child understands a particular form that is significant for functioning in an important life setting, and that form may not appear on the standardized test. Informal assessment gives us the option of testing any form we believe to be important for a particular child. For example, locatives can be evaluated in detail using Procedures 3.4, 3.5, and 3.6 in this book. Standardized tests only test the early acquired forms, *in, on,* and *under.*

To Obtain Accurate Assessments of Children Who Are Difficult to Test

Second, children with other sensory, motor, or behavior disorders may be unable to respond to tests that must be administered in a single prescribed way. Children with severe motor disorders such as cerebral palsy may be unable to point to pictures or engage in other responses neces-

Table 1.3. A sample of standardized tests of comprehension

Test name	Age range	Areas tested
Assessing Semantic Skills Through Everyday Themes (Barrett, Zachman, & Huisingh, 1988)	3–9 years	Receptive and expressive vocabulary in understanding labels; identifying categories, attributes, functions, and definitions; and expressing labels, attributes, functions, and definitions
Boehm Test of Basic Concepts–Preschool (Boehm, 1971)	3–6 years	Basic relational concepts (e.g., space, location, quantity, time, orientation, vocabulary) related to school success
Bracken Basic Concept Scale (BBCS) (Bracken, 1984)	3–7 years	Colors, numbers, letters, shapes, sizes, position, quantity, and social and temporal concepts
Clinical Evaluation of Language Fundamentals–Revised (CELF–R) (Wiig, Second, & Semel, 1992)	5–16 years	Phonology, syntax, semantics, memory, word finding, and word retrieval
Detroit Test of Learning Aptitude–Primary 2 (DTLA–P) (Hammill & Bryant, 1991)	3–9 years	Articulation, conceptual matching, design reproduction, digit sequences, draw-a-person, letter sequences, motor directions, object sequences, oral directions, picture fragments, picture identification, sentence imitation, and symbolic relations
Language Processing Test (LPT) (Richard & Hanner, 1985)	5.11 years	Language processing tasks; associations, categorization, similarities, differences, multiple meanings, attributes, word retrieval difficulties, word substitutions, inability to correct errors, response avoidance, rehearsing responses, and unusual pauses
Lexington Developmental Scale (LDS) and Lexington Developmental Scale Screening Instrument (LDSSI) (Irwin et al., 1973a, b)	Primary grades	Receptive grammar and morphology
MacArthur Communication Development Inventory (Fenson et al., 1993)	8 months–3 years	Parent report of receptive vocabulary and general receptive language
Northwestern Syntax Screening Test (NSST) (Lee, 1971)	3.0–8 years	Receptive syntax
Peabody Picture Vocabulary Test–Revised (PPVT–R) (Dunn & Dunn, 1981)	1.9 years–Adult	Vocabulary
Porch Index of Communicative Ability in Children (PICA–Children) (Porch, 1974)	Birth–6 years	Receptive vocabulary
Preschool Language Scale–3 (PLS–3) (Zimmerman, Steiner, & Pond, 1992)	Birth–7 years	Auditory comprehension
Receptive-Expressive Emergent Language (REEL) Scale (Bzoch & League, 1971)	Birth–3 years	Language skills in infancy, parent report of skills
Receptive One-Word Picture Vocabulary Test (ROWPVT) (Gardner, 1985)	2–12 years	Vocabulary
Reynell Developmental Language Scales (Reynell, 1985)	1–5 years	General receptive skills
Rhode Island Test of Language Structure (RITLS) (Engen & Engen, 1983)	3–20 years with hearing impairment; 3–6 years	Understanding of language structure and receptive syntax

(continued)

Table 1.3.   *(continued)*

Test name	Age range	Areas tested
Sequenced Inventory of Communication Development (SICD) (Hedrick, Prather, & Tobin, 1975)	4 months–4 years	Awareness, discrimination, understanding, expressive behaviors, imitating, initiating, responding, and verbal output
Test of Auditory Comprehension for Language–Revised (TACL–R) (Carrow-Woolfolk, 1985)	3–9.11 years	Vocabulary, morphology, and syntax
Test of Early Language Development (TELD–2) (Hresko, Reid, & Hammill, 1991)	4.0–8.11 years	Receptive/expressive semantics and syntax
Test of Language Development–2 Primary (TOLD–2) (Newcomer & Hammill, 1988)	4–9 years	Vocabulary and syntax
Test of Language Development–Intermediate (TOLD–I) (Newcomer & Hammill, 1988)	8.6–13 years	Vocabulary and syntax
Test of Preschool Language Proficiency (Graham, 1974)	3–8 years	Receptive semantics
Test for the Reception of Grammar (TROG) (Bishop, 1982)	4–12.11 years	Vocabulary and syntax
Test of Relational Concepts (Edmonston & Thane, 1993)	3.0–7.11 years	Dimensional adjectives; spatial, temporal, and quantitative words
Token Test for Children (DiSimoni, 1978)	3–12 years	Receptive syntax
Vocabulary Comprehension Scale (VCS) (Bangs, 1976)	2.6–5 years	Pronouns, quantity, quality, position, direction, size, time, possessives, category words, negation, and functions
Woodcock Language Proficiency Battery–Revised (Woodcock, 1991)	3–80 years	Picture vocabulary, antonyms, synonyms, analogies, letter–word identification, word attack, passage comprehension, dictation, proofing, punctuation, capitalization, spelling, and usage

sary for formal testing. Children with other physical disorders, such as deafness, blindness, paralysis, or multiple disabilities, may also have problems perceiving stimuli or delivering required responses. Children with emotional or behavior problems may be unable or unwilling to cooperate with standard testing procedures. For hard-to-test children with a variety of disabilities, informal procedures become necessary. These procedures that allow flexibility in method of presentation and response are necessary to get a realistic picture of language comprehension, which is, in turn, necessary in order to compare performance in the two language modalities in order to make intervention decisions.

To Assess Comprehension of Children in the Early Stages of Language Development

Third, for children at the emerging language level and in the early part of the developing language stage, few standardized measures exist. Available tests may be inappropriate for youngsters unable to respond to the formality of their procedures. There are not many comprehension tests that have been standardized to assess understanding of grammatical structures in children with language levels in the birth-to-3 period, for example. In addition, children at this level may have very limited vocabularies. They may know some words, but not the words used on the test. They may also be inconsistent in responses and may have difficulty with abstractions such as 2-dimensional pictures. They have fleeting attentional capacities, so that a clinician would need to be able to assess performance by focusing on what attracts the child's attention from moment to moment. Few children at this level can attend consistently to tasks of little inherent interest to them. At these early stages, it is often necessary to use informal procedures to get an idea of the kinds of basic words and sentences the child can understand.

To Examine Discourse-Level Comprehension

Finally, few standardized tests give us a look at that other level of comprehension: the discourse level. Because we know these skills are an equally important piece of the comprehension puzzle, we will want to have some way of assessing them and comparing them with literal comprehension skills. Although there are some standardized tests that look at pragmatic skills, most focus on production. Few allow specific comparisons between literal- and discourse-level skills. Then, too, standardized tests are, by nature, decontextualized. If a child "fails" a standardized test of comprehension, we don't know whether the child might do better on similar forms by applying some strategies in a more friendly, contextualized setting. As mentioned previously, it will be important in planning an intervention program to know whether a contextualized setting helps. If so, such settings can be used as a starting point and gradually faded. If not, some more intensive, broadly based intervention approaches may be necessary.

WHY NOT RELY ON PARENT REPORTS?

But what about parent reports? If we need to know about a child's comprehension, and the child is difficult to test, can't we just ask the parents?

Several parent report measures have been available to clinicians for some time (e.g., *Receptive-Expressive Emergent Language Scale [REEL Scale]* [Bzoch & League, 1971], *Vineland Adaptive Behavior Scales [VABS]* [Sparrow, Balla, & Cicchetti, 1984]). The reliability of measures such as the REEL Scale has been suspect because they depend on parents' retrospective memory of their child's development to complete the scale (e.g., "When did your child say his [or her] first words?" or "When did he [or she] first say two-word sentences?"). A more recent procedure, the *MacArthur Communicative Development Inventories* (CDI) (Fenson et al., 1993) have been designed to overcome this problem by asking parents to report on what their child is doing at the moment, and by providing example vocabulary to check off or example sentences. There are two forms, an infant scale for children 8–16 months of age that contains the comprehension scale, and a second form for toddlers from 16 to 30 months. Despite the high reliability of the CDI, it is important to point out that parent reports of comprehension are more problematic than reports of production, primarily because the child's use of comprehension strategies can fool parents about what the child is understanding.

CHARACTERISTICS OF GOOD INFORMAL ASSESSMENTS

Comprehension procedures will have to be direct, but informal, in presentation. They will need to be flexible in the vocabulary they employ, so that the words the particular child knows can be used. They will need to allow flexibility in order of presentation of items and to allow multiple presentations and repetitions to take developmentally young children's limited attentional capacity into account. They must make it possible to present stimuli in a variety of ways (e.g., using either objects or pictures) and must allow for a variety of response options. Also, they will need to look at a variety of levels of comprehension abilities. Standardized tests are an excellent method of assessing some aspects of literal, decontextualized comprehension at some developmental levels in children who have the motor and attentional skills to respond to them. Informal methods are often needed, though, to assess additional areas of understanding at additional levels of development and for children who lack the ability to respond to formal tests. Provision of these informal methods is the purpose of this book.

THE PROCEDURES IN THIS BOOK

Most of the procedures presented in this volume have a formal structure: Suggestions and instructions for presentation are given, prescribed linguistic and nonlinguistic stimuli are presented, and a specified order of presentation is recommended. Because they are nonstandardized, the procedures do not meet statistical criteria for standardization in terms of norming population sample size and measure of reliability or validity. However, they do allow the flexibility needed to assess comprehension in some children. They do not have to be administered in exactly the form in which they are presented.

Individualization of Procedures

Any procedure in this book can be adapted in any way to meet the needs of an individual child. A variety of modes of presentation (e.g., objects or pictures) can be used. Items can be repeated with intonational changes as required to promote attention, engagement, and responses in individual children. Order of presentation can be changed, except where there is a logical sequence (e.g., Procedure 2.3 must be administered before Procedure 2.4). Timing and modality of response can be adjusted to individual needs. Vocabulary can be selected to maximize chances for success. These procedures are meant to provide a starting point for clinicians, not an end in themselves. Judgment and creativity are encouraged in adapting and modifying the procedures to suit each child's abilities, needs, and interests, and the requirements of the testing context. Such individualization of procedures will require advanced preparation. Planning should include a number of considerations.

Your work setting will be one of the most important issues in planning the administration of procedures for individual children. If you are in a clinic, the populations served may be very diverse and require preparation across developmental levels. At the very least, you will need to become familiar with the full range of procedures found in this volume. Clinics that provide tertiary services may see children only every 6 months or once a year, which has the benefit of allowing comparison to past performance data for both comprehension and production. School settings have a number of advantages, including knowledge of the children through the school year and the opportunity to observe them in classroom contexts. In either setting, take the following steps to optimize your planning. Also note that each of these areas changes as development advances so you will want to take these five steps for the individual child in each developmental level.

1. Review the child's academic record, grade level, referral, or placement in special education programs including speech and language. This will help you determine the child's general cognitive level

when testing data are not available. With these data and the child's chronological age, developmental level can be determined.

2. Identify the child's interests and needs so vocabulary can be identified to optimize performance. This is particularly important in the emerging language stage.

3. Review the child's daily routines with parents, caregivers, and teachers so appropriate content, including vocabulary and discourse contexts, can be selected for use in the procedures.

4. Collect language production data. This may be done directly through a language sample or observation in the waiting room or classroom, or indirectly by interviewing parents and teachers or obtaining a parent report for young children. These data are critical for identifying the initial content of your assessment of comprehension.

5. Review perceptual and motor performance from the child's chart, school records, or direct testing. Knowing the child's hearing and visual acuity levels will help you adapt materials. Also, review visual scanning, and figure ground perception before using picture-based procedures. Motor skills necessary to perform the selected procedures must be established prior to testing. These data will show you which response options are available for each child.

Using these procedures as a guide to informal comprehension assessment will, we hope, lead to a general expansion of the options for comprehension assessment to address the great variety of needs of children with a range of disabilities.

General Preparation for Assessment

In addition to taking steps to individualize the procedures for specific children, some general preparation is necessary. Before testing you will need to identify the response mode(s) available to the child, and the initial content based on the child's production (see the discussion on individualization of procedures and Chapter 5 for examples). Once the child-specific portion of preparation, including identifying the child's developmental level, response capabilities, and language to be assessed, has been completed, then specific procedures must be selected (e.g., picture formats, object formats).

Materials for each procedure must be pulled together, which will take some time. We recommend using a cardboard box for each type of procedure (e.g., locatives in Procedures 3.4 and 3.5) so that all materials needed for this procedure and its adaptations are in one place. The same suggestion applies to the picture-pointing procedures. If you keep all of your pictures and related adaptations together, you will find they can be used over and over again.

After the stimulus materials have been gathered, then it is time to consider how to record responses. Most of the procedures simply require paper-and-pencil notations (e.g., stimuli presented, child responses, marks on score sheet for correct or incorrect). For many of the procedures in this book, sample score sheets are provided. You may wish to use these or to create variations of them. It will add considerably to your information about the child if you record exactly what the child did or said, rather that just noting that the response was correct or incorrect. Patterns of incorrect responses can indicate how the child is approaching the task. Procedure 3.7, for example, includes foils, which are organized to determine if the child is using word order to solve the problem, responding as if the sentence were reversed, or considering the sentence as a list of independent or random words.

Object manipulation procedures offer the best opportunity to observe exactly how the child understands the stimulus sentences, but we must be ready to record the child's responses exactly as they occur. Some of these procedures, such as Procedure 3.2, suggest videotaping where possible. Videotaping can be very useful in maintaining child response data and freeing the examiner to focus only on administering the stimulus items. The disadvantage of videotape is that you must review it to score the data, so you double your time commitment. In addition, placement of the camera is critical to recording all of the child's behavior. We have experimented with videorecording sessions by placing the camera to focus on the table to be used for testing, making sure the whole surface is visible through the lens. When the child arrives, the camera is turned on (because no camera operator is available), and the child generally performs the object manipulation task by raising the items above the table and out of camera range at least half of the time. Obviously, in these experiments the videotape was not very useful and we had to score the items by hand anyway. If the child is amenable, videotaping can be helpful in preserving performance. However, we recommend that you do not use videotaping to put off on-line scoring. Our experience suggests that on-line scoring is best whenever possible.

PRINCIPLES OF INFORMAL COMPREHENSION ASSESSMENT

Both for the procedures presented in this book and for any informal comprehension assessments you may develop independently, there are some general principles that can serve as a guide. These guiding principles are outlined briefly here.

We see the clinical assessment of comprehension as a three-tiered process:

1. *Literal comprehension:* The first task is to evaluate the child's ability to decode the intended literal meaning of words and sentences. This stage of lexical/syntactic assessment is referred to as the literal portion of the comprehension assessment. That is, we will look at both the understanding of words (i.e., lexical) and sentences (i.e., syntactic) as part of our assessment of the literal level. Some procedures will focus specifically on whether or not children understand particular words (i.e., lexical comprehension). When we know whether the individual words are understood, we can combine them into sentences to assess syntactic comprehension (i.e., the ability to derive meaning from the grammatical combination of words). In assessing literal comprehension, every attempt is made to remove all extralinguistic cues, creating a decontextualized listening situation for the child. In this way, a valid statement about the child's understanding of words and sentences themselves, without contextual cues, can be made.

2. *Use of comprehension strategies:* The second phase of comprehension assessment looks at the ways in which the child does use the context in responding to words and sentences beyond his or her linguistic level. To do this, the child's use of strategies, or consistent response biases, is assessed by presenting sentence types that are known, based on the assessment of literal comprehension ability, to go beyond the limit of a child's lexical/syntactic knowledge. Then consistent response preferences are examined. Comparing these strategies to those seen in typically developing children provides a second level of information about the ways in which the child deals with linguistic input.

3. *Discourse features:* The third level of assessment specifically examines the child's ability to deal with the discourse parameters of the language he or she receives.

Using this three-tiered system will, we believe, allow us to get a well-rounded picture of the child's ability to make sense of the language he or she receives. At the same time, it provides the opportunity to define relatively precisely the level at which the child's understanding breaks down—word, sentence, or discourse—so that intervention can be focused appropriately.

How can we assess this complex process, which is not purely linguistic but cognitive and social as well? As in any scientific investigation, it will be necessary, in studying children's language comprehension, to reduce the number of variables that we examine at any given time. Although a division into three tiers is somewhat artificial, it is probably accurate to say that in order to extract meaning from a sentence, at least in a decontextualized situation, it is necessary to understand the meaning of the words in it. Similarly, in order to understand a speaker's intention or draw inferences from a sentence, again in a decontextualized situation, it is necessary to be able to use the syntactic information in the sentence to assign semantic roles such as agent, action, and object of action, and to derive a literal meaning. By examining each of the three phases of comprehension and comparing contextualized and decontextualized performance, it will be possible to get a precise picture of when and how comprehension failures occur and to learn about the strategies the child uses when the linguistic input is too much to handle. Information about all of these aspects of the child's receptive skill can then be compared to the information gathered on his or her language production. With this complete picture of the child's communication, the most appropriate intervention program can be targeted to meet the child's individual needs. For children whose comprehension skills are better than their production skills, production will be the major target of intervention, using their strengths in comprehension as an advantage. Where comprehension and production skills of a specific form or meaning area are problematic, the usual strategy is to combine comprehension and production training. This follows the principle put forward by Lahey (1988) that comprehension training does not necessarily generalize to productive use. If children need work in both modalities, then both need to be targeted in the intervention program.

We can invoke some basic rules while doing informal comprehension assessment across a variety of developmental levels.

Avoid
Overinterpretation

When we use informal procedures to assess comprehension, it is important to remember that we are always inferring something about a private event, and are not observing comprehension directly. This means we must be very careful not to overinterpret what we observe, particularly in contextualized situations. If a child responds appropriately to an instruction such as, "Put the spoon in the cup," we need to remember that there is a bias toward putting things in containers like cups. To know whether the child really comprehends the preposition *in*, we will need to ask the child to put the spoon *in*, for example, a shoe, or something that would be less conventionally expected.

Control
Linguistic Stimuli

When looking at a child's understanding of language, we need to know exactly what we are testing. If we want to look at comprehension of early developing spatial terms, such as the prepositions *in*, *on*, and *under*, it is important to be certain that any other vocabulary items used in the utterance are well known to the child. We would not ask a 3-year-old to "Put the spoon in the left-hand drawer," for example. When testing vocabulary comprehension, we need to have established that all of the other words in the utterance, besides the one being assessed, are familiar. This can be accomplished either by pretesting, or by carefully interviewing the parents about words the child knows.

In the same vein, we need to control the length of sentences used in criterion-referenced comprehension assessment. If we know a child uses only three to four words in his or her own sentences, we should limit the sentence used in the assessment to that length. Furthermore, we need to be careful to test all structures in sentences of equal length. We should not conclude, for example, that a child has difficulty understanding passive sentences if we give him or her "The car was knocked over by the blocks" and "The block pushes the car." The passive sentence is not only more complex but also longer than the active sentence. If the child does not demonstrate comprehension of the passive sentence, we don't know whether length or complexity is the problem. Similarly, if we are testing a structure, we need to be sure that the sentence containing it is as simple as possible, except for the structure being tested. If we were assessing comprehension of possessive markers, for example, we would want to ask the child to "Show me dolly's (or Mommy's) nose," rather than "Show me the car's (or truck's) back wheel." The main point is that when devising informal comprehension assessments, the linguistic stimuli must be thought about very carefully to make sure that we are assessing what we mean to assess.

Specify an
Appropriate Response

When developing informal comprehension assessments, the response is as important as the stimulus. As stated previously, we are always inferring comprehension rather than observing it directly, so what we observe must be considered carefully. Informal comprehension assessments can employ either *naturalistic* or *contrived* responses, but in either case, it is important to specify what response will count as a success so that what we are looking for in the assessment is clear.

Naturalistic responses include *behavioral compliance* and *answers to questions*. Behavioral compliance is an appropriate response to observe in children with developmental levels as young as 12 months. It can include touching, moving, picking up, pointing to, or giving objects, and can be focused on the assessment of single words ("Give me the *shoe*"; "Put it *under* the cup"), morphemes ("This is *Mommy's* cookie"), sentence types ("I *don't* want the spoon"), or speech act intentions ("Can you *open* the box?"). Specifying a naturalistic response does not have to mean that the assessment involves contextualized language. Both contextualized and decontextualized comprehension can be tested in this format. In fact, it is quite important to distinguish between these two conditions when using a naturalistic response. Remember that a very young child can comply with a request stated as a long, complex sentence such as, "Why don't you open this nice box for me?" (Shatz & Gelman, 1973). However, that compliance does not necessarily mean that the child comprehends every aspect of the form. Instead, the child might only recognize the words *open* and *box* and comply because he or she expects adults to ask children to do things. So, unless contextualized and decontextualized variants of a form are contrasted, it will be hard to know whether a child complies with the linguistic stimulus itself, or with what is normally expected in an interactive situation.

Answers to questions are another naturalistic response that can be employed. Usually children will not be reliable in answering questions until after a developmental level of 24 months. Answers to questions can be scored for either semantic or syntactic accuracy. Syntactic accuracy simply involves an answer in the appropriate category. If you ask a child what color an apple is and he says "Blue," this answer is syntactically appropriate, but semantically incorrect. Semantic accuracy involves an answer that would be considered meaningfully accurate by adult standards. Often children can respond with syntactic accuracy before they are entirely semantically correct. Questions, too, can be presented in contextualized conditions, with picture referents or about familiar daily activities. Alternatively, questions can be asked in more decontextualized forms, about events removed from the immediate situation, or about objects and concepts about which the child has only minimal direct experience.

Contrived responses resemble those used in standardized testing. The most common contrived response for a comprehension assessment is *picture pointing*. Children with developmental levels of 24 months or older can generally respond successfully to picture-pointing tasks. Single-word comprehension ("Point to the *shoe*"), understanding of sentences ("Point to 'There are many shoes'"), or inferential comprehension ("Which picture shows what happened next in the story?") can easily be assessed with this format. *Object manipulation* is another contrived response, in which children are asked to do something to a set of objects the clinician presents. A developmental level of approximately 20 months is generally required for a response in this format. Object manipulation procedures can be used to assess understanding of sentences ("Show me, 'The boy is pushed by the girl'"). They can also be used to assess understanding of connected discourse and inferencing ability by asking children to act out what happened in a story or what will happen next.

An additional contrived response that can be used in the criterion-referenced assessment is a *best-fit*, or *judgment*, response. These types of responses involve some metalinguistic abilities in that they require the child to evaluate language, rather than merely use it. As such, they are not appropriate for children younger than 5 years of age. However, for school-age children, judgment responses can be very effective and are easier to construct than picture-pointing or object manipulation tasks. Rather than needing a picture or set of objects to represent each aspect of the stimulus, judgment tasks can involve only two pictures, which the child uses to represent as "right" or "wrong," "OK" or "silly," or some other dichotomy. For example, to assess understanding of passive sentences, the child might be given a picture of an "OK," ordinary-looking lady and a "silly" or clown-like lady. The child can be told to point to the picture of the lady who would say each sentence. After several demonstrations of what each lady might say, (e.g., OK lady: "An apple is eaten by a boy"; Silly lady: "A boy is eaten by an apple"), the child can be asked to judge subsequent sentences. A similar procedure could be used to assess understanding of the connected discourse ("Is it an OK story or a silly story?"), inferencing ("And then he ate the cake. Is that an OK ending or a silly ending?"), speech act intention ("I asked, 'Can you pass the salt?' and he said, 'Yes.' Is that an OK answer or a silly answer?"), speech style variation ("He said to the teacher, 'Give me a pencil.' Is that an OK way to ask?"), and so forth. Table 1.4 provides information on relations between these types of responses and MLU.

Elicit Multiple Responses

Whatever types of responses we elicit, we will need to elicit an adequate number of them. Standardized tests usually have only one or two items to test each structure. It can be hard to tell, then, whether the child's performance is due to chance, particularly in a picture-pointing format where even if the child is pointing randomly, there is a chance of being right. Informal procedures can include more instances for each form being tested.

> **A good rule of thumb is to include at least four examples for each form, and to require the child to get three of the four right in order to succeed on that particular form.**

Another technique is to use contrasting sentence pairs (e.g., "A boy eats a fish" and "A fish eats a boy") and require that the child perform correctly on both elements in the pair. Both of these approaches can minimize the effects of random guessing.

CONCLUSION

Informal procedures such as those described in this book can be fun for both the child and clinician. Because they are flexible and can be adapted to specific interests and abilities, children do not often have a sense of failure on difficult items. If, for example, they use a "child-as-agent" strategy to act out a test item such as, "Make the horse kiss the truck," they don't know that they did not "pass" the item. From their point of view, they are merely participating in a somewhat silly game that allows them to move about instead of sit still, to play with interesting toys instead of looking at pictures, and to interact with a friendly adult instead of obeying an intimidating examiner. In this atmosphere, we have the best chance of observing children's usual responses to lan-

Table 1.4.   A summary of the developmental sequence for each of the four performances, with respect to MLU

MLU	Stage	Production	Comprehension	Judgment	Correction
1.1–1.5	Early Stage I	Correct use of word order in active sentences with semantic constraints	Random performance on acting out reversible active sentence; good comprehension if strong semantic constraints		
1.5–2.0	Late Stage I	Many more three-term (agent-action-object) sentences produced; reversible actives rarely produced	Good comprehension of reversible actives (i.e., use of word-order information alone)		
2.0–2.5	Stage II				
2.5–3.0	Stage III			Unable to judge reversed word order as "wrong"	
3.0–3.5	Early Stage IV		Systematic reversal of reversible passives (i.e., overgeneralization of active word order)	Can judge semantic anomaly but not reversed word order as "wrong"	No corrections
3.5–4.0	Late Stage IV– Early Stage V			Accurate judgments of both semantic anomaly and reversed word order	Corrections of semantic anomaly only; semantic corrections for "wrong" word order sentences
4.0–4.5	Late Stage V		Correct comprehension of reversible passives		Direct word order corrections

Sources: Chapman (1978); Chapman & Miller (1975); de Villiers & de Villiers (1973); Fenson et al. (1993); Owens (1992).

guage, their best responses under controlled conditions, and their least ambiguous reactions to speech. An atmosphere like this will give us the most ideal opportunity to gather data about a child's linguistic knowledge exhibited through auditory comprehension.

2 ◇ Assessing Comprehension in the Emerging Language Stage

Developmental level: 8–24 months
Language level: Brown's stages I–II; Mean length of utterance
   1.0–2.5
Production milestones: At this level, children are producing single words and some early word combinations. Vocabulary
   size is generally small, fewer than 100 words. Few morphological markers are used. Phonological repertoire may
   also be limited, with certain consonants and syllable types
   (consonant-vowel-consonant [CVC], multisyllabic words)
   missing.

Children in the emerging language stage, which corresponds in typical development from about 8 to 24 months of age, understand very little of the language spoken to them. Our task is to document how much true linguistic comprehension is present. In addition, though, we want to examine the extent to which nonlinguistic and discourse-level strategies are used to aid comprehension of more advanced forms. The procedures in this chapter are designed to look at the types of words and word combinations a child can understand, rather than to make a complete catalog of all the words and sentences a child knows. You will try to assess whether the child understands *any* action words, for example, not to develop a list of all the action words the child comprehends.

ADMINISTRATION PROBLEMS THAT MAY ARISE

The administration of these procedures can present clinicians with some unique problems. A discussion of these problems and some suggestions for avoiding them follows.

First, attention at this age is very fleeting. You will need to ensure that the child is attending to the task or objects before scoring the response. Because the procedures are informal, you can repeat items if you believe the child was not attending, but attention will have to be monitored carefully throughout the assessment session.

Second, comprehension strategies can be very misleading as you interpret responses to spoken language throughout this period. Parents and caregivers, in particular, although very reliable in other observations about their children, may mistakenly believe that their youngsters understand everything said to them. In order to focus specifically on linguistic comprehension, you will want to be careful to avoid giving the kinds of nonlinguistic cues children frequently use to derive meaning. Two specific suggestions for avoiding this problem are as follows:

- Be careful not to look at the object you are naming when asking a child to identify it.
- Be sure you are not gesturing toward the object as you name it.

It is easy to give nonverbal cues such as these unconsciously because they are a part of typical interaction with children of this age. When testing for linguistic comprehension, though, you must be careful to eliminate nonverbal cues. If a child fails to respond accurately to the purely linguistic information, we can consciously add the nonverbal cues, giving the same linguistic stimulus, while looking at or gesturing toward an object. If these cues result in improved performance, we can credit the child with a developmentally appropriate strategy, even though the linguistic comprehension is not in evidence. In this way we can begin to document both linguistic and discourse-level comprehension in children with emerging language skills.

Another issue at this developmental level is inconsistency of performance. You will want to ensure that a correct response to any stimulus is not a matter of chance. To make sure, elicit at least two correct responses for each class of items.

In this stage, it is important to determine whether the child understands words only in the context of familiar routines, or also out of context (i.e., a new context for the child or an unlikely situation for the word to appear). So, you will probably want to give the child instructions to carry out in both expected and unexpected settings. You might ask the child to turn the page while reading a book, for example, and to turn the page when an open book is nearby but not being looked at directly. Another contextual issue concerns whether a child can identify objects both within view and when out of sight. If a child can identify an object by name from an array of objects in immediate view, it will also be useful to know whether the child can search for the same object under the table, for example, when its name is mentioned. The ability to find mentioned objects, whether they are absent or present, is a verbal version of object permanence tasks often used to assess nonverbal cognitive status at this level. As such, it is helpful to assess object permanence in a nonverbal format, using procedures like those described by Dunst (1981), in conjunction with this phase of comprehension assessment. In this way, performance on the nonverbal task can be compared to performance on verbal items. If the child is unable to do the nonverbal version of the task, you will be less willing to attribute failure on the verbal activity to a language-specific problem than if the child can perform the nonverbal object permanence tasks, but fails only to search for objects when they are named.

ASSESSMENT GUIDELINES

Normative data collected by Miller et al. (1980) for performance on the procedures in this chapter are given in Table 2.1. Clinically, a child who is passing items that are passed by 75% of children in his or her age group is considered to be doing fine. If the child is not passing items that are passed by 50%–75% of children in his or her age group, you may want to reevaluate comprehension in that child in 2–3 months. If lags are still seen, a comprehension problem may be present.

In assessing discourse-level comprehension during this stage, questions will concern the child's ability to participate in discourse structure, such as turn-taking, and to engage in early topic-sharing activities primarily around joint reference to objects and events. Presuppositional skills are quite primitive at this point, involving primarily the ability to recognize the new or changing aspect of a situation (Greenfield, 1978). However, children in this stage are quite good at deriving illocutionary

Table 2.1. Percentage of children in each age group passing a comprehension item at least once

Comprehension item	Age group (months)			
	10–12	13–15	16–18	19–21
Person name	100	100	92	92
Object name	42	100	100	100
Action verb	8	33	75	83
Absent person or object	0	17	33	67
Possessor-possession	0	8	42	83
Action-object	0	8	42	67
Agent[a]-action	0	0	8	58
Agent[a]-action-object	0	0	0	8

[a]Other than child.

Data from Miller, J.F., Chapman, R.S., Branston, M., & Reichle, J. (1980). Language comprehension in sensorimotor stage V and VI. *Journal of Speech and Hearing Research, 23*(2), 284–311.

intent for requests by using something like a child-as-agent strategy (i.e., interpreting complex remarks as requests for the child to do something) (see Paul [1990] for a review). The discourse comprehension procedures outlined in this chapter are quite informal and are used mainly to investigate whether the child is becoming involved in simple conversational exchanges.

PREPARATION
FOR ASSESSMENT

Remember that the vocabularies of children in this stage are very limited. The vocabulary used in all of the procedures designed for this period of development must be individualized for each child and each procedure. You will want to get a list of words that the child may know from the parent or caregiver. The child's own toys may be most easily recognized, so it may be a good idea to ask parents to bring toys from home to be used in testing. Other familiar items, such as baby dolls, farm animal toys, eating utensils, and familiar clothing items (life- or doll-size) can be added to the assessment materials.

In order to proceed with testing comprehension at the emerging language stage, then, you will need to do the following:

1. Assemble the favorite or familiar toys from the child's home and add some developmentally appropriate objects of which the parents think the child understands the names.
2. Use a comfortable room with a rug, a low child's chair, and an easy chair for lap sitting.
3. Make a list of stimuli you will be using on a score sheet (an example of a score sheet appears on p. 35) to facilitate recording trials and correct responses.
4. Judge each parent's ability to participate in the testing. In most cases, a parent can perform an invaluable role in holding and comforting the child and in making suggestions for altering stimuli or response sets.

Then get down on the floor and get started!

PROCEDURE
2.1 # Comprehension of Familiar Routines

DEVELOPMENTAL LEVEL   8–12 months

LINGUISTIC LEVEL   Lexical

LINGUISTIC STIMULI   Words taken from routine games played regularly by the child and parent or caregiver

RESPONSE TYPE   Natural—behavioral compliance: entering the game when mentioned with appropriate gestures

MATERIALS   None

PROCEDURE

1. Ask parents to demonstrate one of the games they often play with the child (e.g., pat-a-cake, peekaboo, "So Big," "I'm gonna-get-you") without using gestures or motor activities to cue the child.
2. Play more than one game when possible and use appropriate intonation both with and without words to distinguish between intonation and lexical cues.
3. If the child fails to respond to the words for any game, take the opportunity to demonstrate to parents the power of gestures in cuing what appear to be appropriate responses to verbal language.
4. Record responses on a score sheet like the one on page 35.

PASSING RESPONSE   The child enters game(s) at parent's or caregiver's verbal request with appropriate gestures.

PROCEDURE 2.2	◇	# Joint Reference Activity

DEVELOPMENTAL LEVEL

8 months and up

LINGUISTIC LEVEL

Discourse

LINGUISTIC STIMULI

Natural conversation

RESPONSE TYPE

Natural—behavioral compliance

MATERIALS

- Age-appropriate toys

PROCEDURE

1. Have the parent play with toys and talk with the child as he or she might at home.
2. Observe whether the child's attention can be directed to particular objects and activities by the parent's use of speech and gestures. Attention is signaled by looking at the object the parent points out, moving toward it, or acting on it in some way.

Note that the purpose of this procedure is *not* to ascertain whether the child has lexical comprehension of the words the parent uses, but whether the child can use auditory and visual cues to focus attention on objects of common interest. This ability lays the basis for the comprehension strategy examined in Procedure 2.3.

3. Record responses on a score sheet like the one on page 35.

PASSING RESPONSE

The child attends to objects indicated by the parent.

DIAGNOSTIC NOTE

Children with autism often have more difficulty in this area of discourse development than children without autism (Wetherby & Prutting, 1984). Therefore, it is a good diagnostic indicator. If a child shows frequent request functions using nonverbal means (e.g., pulling an adult to an object), but makes very little use of joint attention, autism may be suspected. Children who show joint attentional behavior, however, but are not using verbal means of expression, may have a more specific language disorder.

PROCEDURE 2.3 ◇ Comprehension of Object and Person Names

DEVELOPMENTAL LEVEL	12–18 months
LINGUISTIC LEVEL	Lexical
LINGUISTIC STIMULI	Object names produced by the child or that the parents believe the child knows
RESPONSE TYPE	Natural—attention to objects

MATERIALS

- Toys or objects brought by the parent whose names the child says or may know
- Other common objects, such as a shoe, diaper, bottle, ball, truck, and baby doll
- To test for comprehension of person names, one or two people the child knows (e.g., parent[s], a caregiver)

PROCEDURE

1. Place several of the objects on the floor in front of the child.
2. Get the child's attention by calling his or her name in a loud, sing-song manner.
3. Present the name of the object you want the child to choose in a simple carrier phrase such as, "Where's the shoe?" Use exaggerated intonation to mark the object's name (shoe). Repetition of the carrier phrase is allowed.
4. Repeat the procedure using different objects. Be sure to name an object the child is not already attending to, and be sure not to point to or look at the object you are naming. (This is harder to do than it sounds!) Only those objects on which the child is to act should be visible. In a novel situation, young children may be too distracted if extraneous stimuli are not controlled. Person names may be tested as well, by asking, "Where's Mama?" or by asking the child to indicate other familiar people in the room when the child is looking elsewhere.
5. Record responses on a score sheet like the one on page 35.

PASSING RESPONSE

The child looks at, shows, or gets object named or the child looks at or indicates person named. An appropriate response is repeated in several trials for each object or person name.

RESPONSE STRATEGIES

- Look at what the adults look at
- Act on objects noticed
- Imitate ongoing activities

To avoid being misled by these strategies, be sure not to look at the object being named, or to use any gestures in administering these items.

PROCEDURE 2.4 Comprehension of Action Words

DEVELOPMENTAL LEVEL

12–24 months

LINGUISTIC LEVEL

Lexical

LINGUISTIC STIMULI

Action words that the child produces or the parent thinks the child may know, such as *tickle*, *hug*, *kiss*, *pat*, *smell*, *blow*, *eat*, *throw*, *open*, *close*, and *hit*

RESPONSE TYPE

Natural—behavioral compliance

MATERIALS

- The same objects used in Procedure 2.3
- The same people as in Procedure 2.3

PROCEDURE

1. Complete Procedure 2.3.
2. Place the objects used in Procedure 2.3 on the floor in front of the child.
3. Get the child's attention by calling his or her name in a sing-song manner.
4. Tell the child to perform an action on the object he or she is playing with, such as "kiss it" or "throw it." Use exaggerated intonation to mark the action word (*kiss* or *throw*). Person names may be tested if the child is already attending to someone (e.g., mother) by saying "Pat Mother" or "Tickle Mother."

Be sure the action the child is asked to perform on the available objects is unconventional; otherwise the child may appear to comprehend the verb by using the "do what you usually do with this object" strategy. Stimuli and commands may be repeated in this procedure also. Because only single-word comprehension is being tested, unconventional actions may be requested on objects. For example, if the child is playing with a book, you may say, "kiss it" or "throw it," but avoid asking the child to perform a conventional action such as "open it."

5. Record responses on a score sheet like the one on page 35.

PASSING RESPONSE

The child performs the action requested. The response is repeated in several trials at different times in the testing session with intervening items.

RESPONSE STRATEGY

- "Do what you usually do" (i.e., conventional use of objects)

DEVELOPMENTAL NOTE

Children in this developmental stage often know more object than action words.

PROCEDURE
2.5   ◇    Comprehension of Words
for Absent Persons and Objects

DEVELOPMENTAL LEVEL   18–24 months

LINGUISTIC LEVEL   Lexical

LINGUISTIC STIMULI   Object names produced by the child that the parents believe the child knows

RESPONSE TYPE   Natural—attention to objects

MATERIALS

- Toys or objects brought by the parent whose names the child says or may know
- Other common objects, such as a shoe, diaper, bottle, ball, truck, and baby doll
- To test for comprehension of person names, one or two people the child knows (e.g., parent[s], a caregiver)

PROCEDURE

1. Complete Procedure 2.3.
2. Choose words the child has responded to successfully in Procedure 2.3.
3. Place the child so some of the familiar objects and people are hidden from view (e.g., behind the child, behind the examiner).
4. Request object or person identification as in Procedure 2.3 (e.g., "Where's the shoe?", "Where's Mama?").
5. Record responses on a score sheet like the one on page 35.

PASSING RESPONSE   The child searches for object or person named. He or she may then get, give, or show the object. If an absent person is out of the room, the child may look or go to the door, or possibly cry at being unable to find the person named. Response is repeated in several trials.

PROCEDURE
2.6 ◇ Comprehension of
Early Two-Word Relations

DEVELOPMENTAL LEVEL   18–24 months

LINGUISTIC LEVEL   Syntactic

LINGUISTIC STIMULI   Person, object, and action words combined to express the following semantic relations:
Possessor-Possession (e.g., *Mommy's shoe*)
Action-Object (e.g., *Kiss the truck!*)
Agent-Action with child as agent (e.g., *Maria, jump!*)
Agent-Action-Object (e.g., *Maria, kiss the truck!*)

RESPONSE TYPE   Natural—behavioral compliance

MATERIALS
- Toys or objects brought by the parent whose names the child says or may know
- Other common objects, such as a shoe, diaper, bottle, ball, truck, and baby doll
- To test for comprehension of person names, one or two people the child knows (e.g., parent[s], a caregiver)

PROCEDURE
1. Choose objects and actions for which the child has demonstrated comprehension in Procedures 2.3 and 2.4.
   Possessor-Possession: Ask the child, "Where's Mama's shoe?" versus "Where's (child's) shoe?"; "Where's (child's) nose?" versus "Where's Mama's nose?"
   Action-Object: Ask the child to perform an unconventional action on an object he or she is not already attending to. For example, if the child is holding a doll, say "Kiss the truck," rather than "Kiss the doll."
   Agent-Action and *Agent-Action-Object with the child as agent:* Ask the child to perform an action ("Sally, jump!") or an action on an object ("Sally, bite the doll!") to which the child is not already attending.
2. Record responses on a score sheet like the one on page 35.

PASSING RESPONSE   The child responds correctly to both elements in the instruction. The response is repeated in several trials.

32

RESPONSE STRATEGIES
- Locate objects mentioned
- Give evidence of notice
- "Do what you usually do" (i.e., conventional action)
- "Child as agent" (i.e., child acts on objects or persons in the way mentioned)

| PROCEDURE 2.7 | | # Turn-Taking in Discourse |

DEVELOPMENTAL LEVEL

18 months and up

LINGUISTIC LEVEL

Discourse

LINGUISTIC STIMULI

Conversation to child

RESPONSE TYPE

Natural—responding when spoken to

MATERIALS

• Appropriate play materials

PROCEDURE

Observe the child engaged in play with a parent or familiar adult for 10–15 minutes.

RECORDING

1. On a score sheet like the one on page 36, record the number of child-directed utterances produced by the adult that would be expected to elicit a verbal response (i.e., questions and comments directed to the child).
2. Record the number of child responses.

For the purpose of this analysis, it is not necessary to record the *content* of the adult's remark or the child's response. Here we only want to know whether the child understands his or her conversational obligation to respond to speech with speech. This analysis can, then, be done on line by keeping a tally of adult utterances and child responses:

Adult's child-directed utterances: ⅢⅡ ⅢⅡ ⅢⅡ ⅢⅡ ⅠⅠ = 22

Child's verbal responses: ⅢⅡ Ⅰ = 6

If the conversation is recorded, it may be transcribed and the content analyzed, if needed. Alternatively, the percentage of contingent responses can be analyzed using a score sheet like the one on page 36.

3. To derive the percentage of times the child fulfills conversational obligation, divide the number of child responses by the number of adult remarks.
4. Compare this percentage to normative data from Bloom, Rocissano, and Hood (1976) for children between 25 and 36 months of age (see data on the score sheet on p. 36 and Procedure 3.2).

DIAGNOSTIC NOTE

Children at this level are not expected to respond to *all* remarks addressed to them, but they should respond to some. By the late preschool to early school years they should respond to most. In adult conversation, failure to respond when spoken to is considered a serious breach of politeness.

<table>
<tr><td>FOR USE WITH
PROCEDURES:
2.1   2.4   3.3
2.2   2.5   3.7
2.3   2.6</td></tr>
</table>

◇ # SCORE SHEET
Assessing Comprehension of Words and Simple Sentences

Instructions: This form is designed as a summary form to record responses across procedures. It may be amended to meet your individualized needs (e.g., you may wish to record many more responses for each procedure). As it appears here, you may record responses in four trials by indicating the word(s) the adult uses as linguistic stimuli under "vocabulary used" and scoring the child's responses for each trial. Use the key below.

Child's name: _____

Child's chronological age (years.months): _____

Date: _____

Procedure	Developmental level (months)	Linguistic structure being tested	Vocabulary used	Responses			
				1	2	3	4
2.1	8–12	Lexical structure within routine game					
2.2	8 and up	Joint reference activity					
2.3	12–18	Lexical comprehension of object and person names outside of routine					
2.4	12–24	Lexical comprehension of action words outside of routine					
2.5	18–24	Lexical comprehension of words for absent persons and objects					
2.6	18–24	Syntactic comprehension of early two-word relations					
3.3	24–48	Syntactic comprehension of two- and three-word relations with toys as agents					
3.7	30–60	Syntactic comprehension of word order					

Scoring key: ✓ = Correct response
            X = Incorrect response (note strategy used, if any)
            NR = No response

The Clinical Assessment of Language Comprehension
by Jon F. Miller and Rhea Paul   © 1995 Paul H. Brookes Publishing Co., Baltimore

<table>
<tr><td>FOR USE WITH
PROCEDURE:
2.7</td><td>◇</td><td>SCORE SHEET
Assessing Turn-Taking
in Discourse</td></tr>
</table>

Instructions: Following the example in Procedure 2.7, tally the adult's child-directed utterances and the child's verbal responses. If desired, compute the percentage of times the child fulfills conversational obligation. Compare this percentage to the data in the table below.

Child's name: _____

Child's chronological age (years.months): _____

Date: _____

Adult utterances versus child responses tally	Total
Adult's child-directed utterances:	
Child's verbal responses:	

Optional computation:

Percentage of times child fulfills conversational obligation (divide the total number of child's verbal responses by the number of adult's child-directed utterances):

_____ %

Average distribution of topic continuations in children's utterances

Average age (months)	Average MLU	Contingent responses (%)	Imitative responses (%)	Total contingent + imitative responses (%)
21	1.26	21	18	39
25	2.60	33	6	39
36	3.98	46	2	48
46	4.45	96	2	98

Source: Bloom, Rocissano, & Hood (1976).

The Clinical Assessment of Language Comprehension
by Jon F. Miller and Rhea Paul   © 1995 Paul H. Brookes Publishing Co., Baltimore

3 ◇ Assessing Comprehension in the Developing Language Stage

Developmental level: 24–60 months
Language level: Brown's stages III–V; Mean length of utterance 2.5–4.5
Production milestones: During this stage, children are acquiring the basic vocabulary and syntax of language. Vocabulary size is expanding rapidly. Morphological markers are beginning to be used in speech. A variety of sentence forms, such as questions and negatives, are beginning to contain appropriate syntactic marking. Toward the end of the stage, complex sentences begin to be used. Phonological simplification processes may interfere with intelligibility.

The developing language stage covers the period when typically developing children are between approximately 2 and 5 years of age. During this time, the child is acquiring language rapidly, producing and understanding an increasing number of words in more complex and elaborated sentences, and expressing a wider variety of meanings on topics increasingly remote from the immediate context in time and space. It has been estimated that children in this period learn six to eight new words a day. At the end of this stage, the child should understand simple sentence forms as well as some conjoined and complex sentence types (Table 3.1). As linguistic learning advances, the variety of discourse situations that can be sampled also expands to include not only dyadic conversation, but also pretend play, story telling, and extended descriptions and explanations.

SPECIAL ASSESSMENT CONSIDERATIONS FOR THE DEVELOPING LANGUAGE STAGE

Children at developmental levels corresponding to 24–60 months of age have only somewhat longer attention spans than their peers in the emerging language stage. They will still need help in the form of reinforcement to persist with assessment activities. Many clinicians use edible reinforcements to keep children focused during this stage. Unfortunately, however, if you need to do several procedures, the child may tire of eating Froot Loops (or whatever reinforcer you have chosen) before you have finished. Token reinforcement, such as checkmarks given for each response, which are traded in for a sticker or treat when 10 are accumulated, are often too abstract or too long-deferred for children in this stage. For most children, a careful mix of praise or social reinforcement and small tangible reinforcers (e.g., stickers; colored paper clips; inexpensive, small toys) will be necessary. A clinician might, for example, praise a child for every few responses made. (Praising for every

Table 3.1.   Examples of sentence types used in the developing language period

Simple sentences—those that contain only one clause or main verb

I like ice cream.	The girl is running.
He went fishing.	The animals frightened the children.
We helped the fire fighters with their hoses.	Two boys in my class watched the game on TV.

Conjoined sentences—those with two or more independent clauses joined by a conjunction (e.g., *and, but, so, or*)

I can eat pizza and drink juice.	Malcolm likes apple pie, but Keri likes cherry.
We can go to the movies or rent a video.	She wants a new bike, so she babysits on weekends.

Complex sentences—those that contain one or more dependent clauses

She wants to be a doctor.	Joy knows what Alex wants for his birthday.
They asked us to move out of their way.	Jamaal has the kind that I want.
I think I'll go swimming.	I wonder how to fix this.

response will become nonreinforcing; keep the reinforcement intermittent or sporadic.) It is important, by the way, to provide this praise whether or not the response is correct. It is important to reinforce responding itself to keep the child focused, rather than to encourage thinking of responses as right or wrong. Interspersed with praise, you might occasionally give the child a colored paper clip. The clips collected during the assessment can be strung together to make a "necklace" that the child may keep or give to his or her mother.

THE EARLY AND LATE SEGMENTS OF THE DEVELOPING LANGUAGE STAGE

For the purpose of assessing comprehension, this stage can be divided into two periods: what might be called the "early" segment of the developing language stage, and the "late" segment. The early segment would correspond in typical development to the period from about 2 to 3½ years, in productive development from MLUs of 2.0–3.5, Brown's stages II–III. This is the period of basic simple sentence development. The later phase would cover roughly from 3½ to 5 years in typical language acquisition, when MLUs are between 3.5 and 4.5, Brown's stages III–V. During this time, complex sentences typically begin to appear. When doing comprehension assessment with a child in the developing stage of productive language, you will probably want to start with the procedures for assessing comprehension in the early segment of this stage, such as Procedures 3.1–3.9. If the child performs accurately on these assessments, you can go on to evaluate comprehension skills of the later segment of this level, such as Procedures 3.10–3.13, regardless of the child's language production ability. Table 3.2 summarizes the early and late segments of this stage.

As the discussion of response modes in Chapter 1 indicates, some new options become available during this stage. In addition to behav-

Table 3.2.   Early and late segments of comprehension assessment in the developing language period

Early	Late
Understanding locatives	Understanding preparatory or sincerity conditions for speech acts
Answering questions	
Understanding intent	Recognizing politeness
Inferring and continuing topics	Understanding requests for clarification
Understanding two- and three-word instructions	
Understanding word order	

ioral compliance, to which we are restricted in the emerging language stage, children can also be asked to answer questions, point to pictures, and manipulate objects. In the later segment of the developing language stage, even some best-fit, or judgment, tasks can be used. However, you need to be careful. Children are still inconsistent about responding to questions until after 3 years of age. You will probably need to restrict using question/answer procedures to the later segment of this developmental period. Responses on picture-pointing tasks are fairly unreliable until the fourth year (see the *Peabody Picture Vocabulary Test–Revised [PPVT]* reliability data [Dunn & Dunn, 1981]), so again we will probably not want to rely on these very much until the later segment of the period. Furthermore, attention span limits the depth of testing on object manipulation tasks in the third year of life. As a result, you will need to be careful to elicit several responses for each item being tested with object manipulation to be sure the response is stable and not a matter of chance. You will also have to intersperse the comprehension testing with other activities to maintain the child's attention. For example, you might administer one comprehension assessment procedure (e.g., Procedure 3.7) and then you might give the child farm toys to play with while you observe vocal behavior during play as part of production assessment. After 5 minutes, you might begin Procedure 3.8, asking conversational questions as the child continues to play with the farm toys.

As noted previously, comprehension strategies continue to play a role during this period. Again, contrasting performance in contextualized and decontextualized administration of the same item will help you to see strategies in operation. If a child is attempting to process the three-term instructions used in these procedures (e.g., "Show me: 'The mommy feeds the baby'") by employing a child-as-agent strategy and performing actions on objects him- or herself consistently (i.e., child feeds the baby doll), this child is probably still operating in the emerging language stage of comprehension and is not ready for the procedures in this chapter.

Although children in the early segment of the developing language stage can, unlike children in the emerging language stage, process all three terms in an agent-action-object sequence (e.g., "The boy pushes the car"), they are still limited in their comprehension of sentences with inanimate, and therefore improbable, agents. Given such a sentence to act out with toys, such as "Show me: 'The boat hits the girl,'" the child in the developing stage will not be able to use the order of the words in the sentence to assign agent (first noun = agent) and object (last noun = object) roles, but will rely on a "probable events" response strategy by making the animate noun the agent, and demonstrating, "The girl hits the boat." Similarly, in sentences with both animate agents and objects (e.g., "The car pushes the truck"), where probable events response strategies do not help, children in this early period are likely to perform at chance levels (i.e., they will be correct half of the time and incorrect half of the time, as if they were guessing) (Chapman & Miller, 1975). Procedure 3.7 tests these reversible types of sentences specifically to evaluate children's ability to use word order to assign semantic relations in sentences. In using Procedure 3.3, though, which tests a more basic level of comprehension involving simply the ability to comprehend all three terms in an agent-action-object sequence, it is important to remember to use animate nouns as agents of action in the test sentences (e.g., "Make the baby pat the truck"). Objects of action should be inanimate. These semantically irreversible sentences are the earliest three-word instructions children would be expected to comprehend during this stage, and comprehension of three terms in a sequence is all you are trying to assess in Procedure 3.3. If the child performs adequately on these earlier-acquired forms, testing can proceed to the more complex reversible sentences in Procedure 3.7.

The early segment of the developing language stage is also a time of important changes in discourse skill. Children begin to understand their conversational obligation to respond to speech with speech, or to speak when spoken to. Although this skill is emerging in the developing language phase, children are not completely reliable about fulfilling their conversational obligations. Reliability of responses both to statements and questions increases throughout the third year. Both are more reliable after age 3 (Owens, 1992). Children are also learning to maintain a conversational topic. They are better, though, at maintaining their own topics than those introduced by others. Even 4-year-olds have trouble continuing a topic for more than a few turns, and repetition is often used as a strategy for topic maintenance by preschoolers (Brinton & Fujiki, 1989). Assessment of discourse comprehension in the developing language stage involves monitoring the development of these skills by assessing their presence in unstructured conversation. For children with disorders that primarily affect production (e.g., cerebral palsy), you could expect that discourse-level skills would be in advance of syntactic level. Even nonverbal or minimally verbal children should be able to demonstrate their understanding of these rules using vocal or gestural means if their difficulties are limited to the productive modality (Paul & Shiffer, 1991). Children who have problems in both lexical/syntactic comprehension and production will be more likely to have difficulties in the development of these discourse-level abilities.

Although the knowledge of their conversational obligation to answer questions develops early, children learn gradually what specific information is requested by particular question words. When they have not yet learned the meaning of a question word, children in the developing language stage will often use the response strategy of "supplying the missing information." However, the question words that the child fails to comprehend will decrease through this period in a predictable order. Comprehension of prepositions develops in a similar fashion. Both of these sequences of development are probably related to the conceptual difficulty of the words involved. The order of acquisition of both *wh-*words and locative prepositions appears to reflect the complexity of the concept expressed (e.g., *what* is understood before *when; in* is understood before *beside*).

As development proceeds in the preschool years, children are able to make increasingly greater use of linguistic information in understanding, learning, and thinking. As a result, they rely less on context and response strategies than they did previously, although these forces will still be operating to a limited extent. For example, during this period children begin to understand the meaning of the order in which words appear in a sentence and begin to be able to differentiate between commands such as:

"Make the boy push the girl"

and

"Make the girl push the boy."

However, sentence types, such as passives, that are exceptions to the normal "first noun-verb-second noun = agent-action-object" formula, can cause problems. Children in the later segment of the developing language stage will often misinterpret such sentences to mean "first noun = agent, last noun = object." As a result, they may misunderstand a passive sentence such as:

"The baby is fed by the mommy"

to mean

"Baby feeds Mommy,"

even though this meaning is contrary to probable events. Such a strategy, although still leading to some misinterpretation, is evidence that children are focusing more sharply on linguistic, as opposed to contextual and prior knowledge, cues during this phase.

Many children in the later segment of the developing language stage will be able to respond to standardized language comprehension testing, using instruments like those listed in Table 1.2. At this level, the purpose of informal assessment includes a more in-depth look at structures the child appeared to fail on the standardized measures, the ability to contrast performance on the decontextualized test with performance in a more contextualized administration, and the ability to examine a broader range of structures than may be addressed by the test. The procedures presented in this chapter can be adapted for testing a variety of forms. The only limits are the developmental data available and your imagination.

Although the most rapid syntactic development takes place during the early developing language period, the phase at the end of this stage is a time of very rapid and dramatic increases in discourse-level skills. In terms of discourse comprehension, major acquisitions include the understanding of preparatory and sincerity conditions for speech acts, increasing sophistication in processing and responding to requests for clarification, and increasing presuppositional and inferential abilities (Chapman, 1981). These abilities are examined in Procedures 3.10–3.13.

PREPARATION
FOR ASSESSMENT

In order to proceed with testing at the developing language level, you will need to have done the following:

1.   Obtain a list of object names and action words for which the child has demonstrated comprehension by pretesting the words to be used in the assessment, using procedures like those discussed in Chapter 2. It is good practice to document comprehension for every individual word you plan to use in testing multiword stimuli.
2.   Collect the objects required to represent the words in the sentences you plan to use. Objects should be of equal size to avoid size as a possible influence in determining agent (e.g., a "large objects act on smaller objects" strategy).

3. Prepare a score sheet to include the linguistic stimuli you are planning to use and a space for recording what the child actually did in response, as well as whether the response was correct or not. (Examples are provided for several procedures in this chapter.) These data will allow you to determine the response strategies the child is using to solve the processing problems posed by the sentences.

4. Select a range of reinforcers, from social to tangible, to maintain the child's attention. Change reinforcers often. Try making "deals" with children who are reluctant to respond. Tell them they will get a "prize" (i.e., a small toy or treat) every 5 or 10 responses. Let them count the responses on their own fingers to make the counting more concrete.

5. Prepare alternate procedures to introduce as the child's attention shifts. When the child tires of the comprehension task, go on to another aspect of the assessment, such as collecting a speech or behavior sample, or evaluating oral-motor skill in an eating activity (see Paul [1995] for detailed procedures for assessing oral-motor and feeding skills). Return later to finish the comprehension task when the child is refreshed. Alternating tasks is the most effective way to maintain motivation.

PROCEDURE 3.1 ◇ Understanding Illocutionary Intent in Indirect Requests in Discourse

DEVELOPMENTAL LEVEL	24–36 months
LINGUISTIC LEVEL	Discourse
LINGUISTIC STIMULI	Requests containing familiar vocabulary in complex syntactic contexts
RESPONSE TYPE	Natural—behavioral compliance
MATERIALS	• Age-appropriate toys for which the child has already demonstrated comprehension in Procedure 2.4
PROCEDURE	1. Choose objects and actions for which the child has already demonstrated comprehension in Procedure 2.4.
	2. As the child plays with toys, periodically embed probable action-object instructions in polite question requests such as, "Would you please pat the doll for me?", "Could you push this car for me?", and "Would you mind tickling this cow?"
	3. Record the child's responses on a score sheet like the one on page 122.
PASSING RESPONSE	The child complies with several complex probable instructions.

PROCEDURE	⟡	# Providing

PROCEDURE 3.2 ⟡ Providing Contingent Responses

DEVELOPMENTAL LEVEL	24–36 months
LINGUISTIC LEVEL	Discourse
LINGUISTIC STIMULI	Natural conversation
RESPONSE TYPE	Natural—conversational replies
MATERIALS	• Age-appropriate toys • Video camera (optional)

PROCEDURE

1. Videotape or observe a 10-minute play interaction between parents and child.
2. For each parent utterance, code the following child response on a score sheet like the one on pages 123–124 as *contingent* (relevant to the topic of the parent's remark), *noncontingent* (irrelevant responses and no responses), or *imitative* (responses that repeat all or part of the parent's utterance). It is not necessary to transcribe the utterances if only contingent responses are being scored. Simply place a tally mark (|) for each adult utterance that attempts to elicit a response from the child.
3. Compute the percentage of contingent and imitative responses and compare to the Bloom, Rocissano, and Hood (1976) data provided on the score sheet on page 124.

Bloom et al. reported that topic continuation increases from 39% to 98% from 21 to 46 months of age. Continuations that include new information (i.e., that are not imitations) increase from 21% to 46% in this period (see the table on p. 124 for Bloom et al. data). Based on the rapid change in children's contingent speech during this developmental period, this procedure may be a particularly sensitive discourse development measure.

PASSING RESPONSE

Children who show levels of contingent responses similar to those in the Bloom et al. data, even if their speech is delayed, are demonstrating positive discourse development. This suggests that their chances for eventually developing good communicative ability are good. Children who have production delays and demonstrate reduced topic continuation skills may be at greater risk for long-term problems.

Comprehension of Two- and Three-Word Instructions with Toys as Agents

DEVELOPMENTAL LEVEL	24–48 months
LINGUISTIC LEVEL	Syntactic
LINGUISTIC STIMULI	Agent-action and agent-action-object relations with an agent other than the child specified
RESPONSE TYPE	Contrived—object manipulation

MATERIALS

- Toys or objects brought by the parent whose names the child says or may know
- Other common objects, such as a shoe, diaper, bottle, ball, truck, baby doll, puppets, and toy animals (This should include items that can serve as agents of actions.)

PROCEDURE

1. Plan to use vocabulary from Procedures 2.3 and 2.4 for which the child has demonstrated comprehension.
2. Familiarize the child with names for the new "agent" toys, and check the child's knowledge of these names.
3. Have several objects available from which the child must choose.
4. Ask the child to act out the instruction such as:

horse eat	doll kiss comb
cow drink	horse eat spoon
doll comb	doll kick cup
horse run	cow throw comb
doll eat	horse hit cup

Instructions should be presented in a simple carrier phrase, such as "Make the horse eat," or "Show me: 'The doll kisses the comb.'" Three-word instructions should *not* be semantically reversible.
5. Record responses on a score sheet like the one on page 125.

PASSING RESPONSE

The child chooses the correct agent from the array and uses it to perform the mentioned action. For three-word instructions, the correct agent and object must be chosen and the appropriate action demonstrated on the object. Responses should be repeated over several trials.

RESPONSE STRATEGIES

- "Child-as-agent"(i.e.,child acts on objects him- or herself in the way mentioned)
- "Do what you usually do" (i.e., conventional use of objects)
- "Probable event"

The latter two strategies listed above may be identified only at the end of testing when the pattern of responses also is identified.

PROCEDURAL NOTE

The data collected from this procedure can be added to those gathered in Procedures 2.1–2.6 to get a cumulative picture of developing sentence comprehension. If the child passes most of the irreversible three-word items tested here, assessment can go on with Procedure 3.7 to examine more complex word-order comprehension tasks. If the child does not pass any three-word items, it is unlikely that he or she will be successful with the word-order items in Procedure 3.7. The clinician should not administer Procedure 3.7 to this child.

PROCEDURE
3.4 ◇ # Comprehension of Locatives: Search Task

DEVELOPMENTAL LEVEL	30–48 months
LINGUISTIC LEVEL	Lexical
LINGUISTIC STIMULI	Prepositions *in, on, under, behind, in front of,* and *beside*
RESPONSE TYPE	Natural—behavioral compliance
MATERIALS	• Toy mailbox or egg carton for reference object • Six small boxes and six raisins, peanuts, or small candies • A piece of cardboard for use as a screen

PROCEDURE

1. Place the six small boxes in the six locative positions (indicated by the prepositions above) relative to the toy mailbox.
2. Introduce the toy mailbox and the screen to the child.
3. Give the child the following instructions: "Here is a raisin (or peanut or candy). I'm going to hide it and I'll tell you where to find it."
4. Put up the screen between the child and the test items.
5. Hide one raisin (or peanut or candy) under the small box *in* the mailbox.
6. Remove the screen.
7. Tell the child, "The candy is in the mailbox."
8. Record the child's response on a score sheet like the one on page 126. Normative data from Hodun (1975) appear there.
9. Put the screen up again and repeat the procedure using the next stimulus locative. The stimulus locatives must be presented in the following order: *in, on, under, behind, in front of, beside.* Because the first three locatives are the easiest, they are presented first to ensure some success. Alter the stimulus sentence as appropriate for each locative preposition.

PASSING RESPONSE

The child finds the prize (raisin, peanut, or candy) under the appropriate box. Response is repeated on several trials with different target objects.

RESPONSE STRATEGY

• "Probable location" (i.e., child searches for objects where they are usually found)

DEVELOPMENTAL NOTE

Although *in, on,* and *under* are understood by 50%–85% of children at 30 months of age, *in front of* and *beside* are not comprehended by most children until 42 months (Hodun, 1975). Hodun (1975) reports that this search task is easier for children than the placement task (see Procedure 3.5).

PROCEDURE
3.5 # Comprehension of Locatives: Placement Task

DEVELOPMENTAL LEVEL	30–48 months
LINGUISTIC LEVEL	Lexical
LINGUISTIC STIMULI	Prepositions *in*, *on*, *under*, *behind*, *in front of*, and *beside*
RESPONSE TYPE	Natural—behavioral compliance
MATERIALS	• Two toys that can serve as agents (e.g., stuffed animals) • Small toys, candies, or raisins • A small bag • Large fronted reference object(s) with suitable hiding places for all prepositions listed, such as mailbox, stove, desk, money box, truck, or jeep

PROCEDURE

1. Give the child instructions similar to the following:

   "I would like you to play a game with me. Here, meet my two friends, Pinky (toy hippo) and Red (toy dog). Let's play with my friends and the toys over here (next to reference objects). Do you know what these are called? That's right, this is a mailbox, a stove, a desk, a money box, a truck, and a jeep. (The child's own names for the objects are used throughout the procedure wherever these differ from the ones originally assigned.) I'll show you how to play this game with my friends. See Pinky? He wants to go in the truck. Put Pinky in the truck. Thank you. That's where he wanted to go. Let's play again. Here's Pinky...."

   Include in the instructions improbable locations to differentiate response strategies from comprehension. Test *in*, *on*, and *under* first, giving at least three test items for each preposition. If the child is consistently successful, contrive to test each of the other terms, also giving three trials for each. If the child is unsuccessful on two of three of the first three prepositions tested, discontinue testing.

2. Record responses on a score sheet like the one on page 126. Use the scoring key on the score sheet to simplify the process. If the child's response is incorrect, note the number of the preposition where the child did place the object. For example, if the child was told to place the object *beside* the mailbox and he or she placed it *in* the mailbox, record X1 in the box for that trial. These notes will allow the clinician to review the score sheet for patterns of response strategies later. Normative data from Hodun (1975) appear on the score sheet on page 126.

PASSING RESPONSE

The child consistently places objects correctly according to the preposition named in the instruction.

RESPONSE STRATEGY

• "Probable location" (i.e., child puts objects in containers and on surfaces)

48

Comprehension of Locatives: Body Placement Task

DEVELOPMENTAL LEVEL	30–48 months
LINGUISTIC LEVEL	Lexical
LINGUISTIC STIMULI	Prepositions *in, on, under, behind, in front of,* and *beside*
RESPONSE TYPE	Natural—behavioral compliance

MATERIALS

- A large wooden or cardboard box with the cover attached to one side to mark the front (reference object)

PROCEDURE

1. Place the box about 6 feet from the child with its front facing him or her.
2. Tell the child, "Let's play a game. I'll tell you where to hide. Go in the box."
3. Record the response on a score sheet like the one on page 126.
4. Repeat the procedure using the next locative. The stimulus locatives must be provided in the following order: *in, on, under, behind, in front of, beside.*

PASSING RESPONSE

The child moves to the appropriate position. Response is repeated in several trials.

RESPONSE STRATEGY

- "Probable location" (i.e., child searches for objects where they are usually found)

Word Order Comprehension

DEVELOPMENTAL LEVEL	30–60 months
LINGUISTIC LEVEL	Syntactic
LINGUISTIC STIMULI	Subject-verb (S-V), verb-object (V-O), subject-prepositional phrase (S-PP), subject-verb-object (S-V-O) reversible sentences, subject-verb-prepositional phrase (S-V-PP) reversible sentences, and verb-object-prepositional phrase (V-O-PP) reversible sentences (Stimulus sentences for this procedure are listed on p. 54.)
RESPONSE TYPE	Pointing to pictures
MATERIALS	• Twenty-nine stimulus plates (see pp. 56–113) of four line drawings each (The first 5, plates A–E, pretest the 20 vocabulary items used in this procedure; the remaining 24 plates are testing stimuli, with one test sentence for each plate.)
PROCEDURE	The clinician may either sit across from or next to the child. What is important is that the child can easily see all four line drawings on the plates and the clinician can see the child's response and record it. The child's comfort is an important consideration. As the clinician administers the stimulus items, he or she must be sure not to cue the child by looking at the correct line drawing. All stimulus items should be read in a consistent tone; no words should be stressed.

Pretest

1. To ensure that the child knows the vocabulary items in this test, using plates A–E, ask the child to point to the stimulus words represented by each picture.
2. For each plate, name the stimulus words in the order specified on the practice plate to ensure that each picture location is sampled equally.
3. Record the picture to which the child points in response to each item as 1–4 on a score sheet like the one on page 52. The child must respond correctly to all the words in this portion of the assessment in order to proceed with testing.
4. After the child has demonstrated knowledge of each vocabulary item, proceed to the test sentences.

Test

1.   For each plate, read the stimulus item and ask the child to point to the picture that matches the item. You may give the child a second chance to respond if no response is given to the first presentation of the stimulus sentence.
2.   Record the child's responses as 1–4 on a score sheet like the one on page 52.
3.   Interpret the data recorded on the score sheet by using the interpretation form on page 53. Each recorded response, whether it is correct or incorrect, tells you something about the child's comprehension strategies relative to understanding word order.

Data Analysis

The score sheet on page 52 and the interpretation form on page 53 are intended to the used together for data analysis. As indicated, the first column of the interpretation form simply lists the plates in order by number. The second column provides the correct answer for each plate. For example, the correct picture on Plate 13 illustrates:

"Mommy's kissing Daddy."

The third column identifies the plate representing the reversed version of the sentence. Consistently reversed responses indicate that the child interprets the utterance in reversed order from that mentioned in the stimulus sentence. For the example above, the reversed response is:

"Daddy's kissing Mommy."

The fourth column identifies the picture representing the vocabulary items in the stimulus sentence unrelated to each other. Children preferring this interpretation understand the words presented but as unrelated items or a list, rather than representing relational meaning. For the example above, the child might choose pictures illustrating Daddy by himself, Mommy by herself, or the boy and girl kissing.

The fifth column identifies the picture representing a major constituent substitution, such as the subject or verb of the sentence. Consistent choices of this type suggest a failure to remember the major constituents of the stimulus sentence. Each of the incorrect, or foil, pictures has been designed to identify alternative approaches children may use prior to understanding word order as a cue to sentence meaning. For example, children may understand sentences as the same, regardless of the word order, selecting both correct and reversed pictures equally often. They may understand the stimulus sentence as a list of independent words, selecting the independent foil. Or, finally, they may fail to remember all of the vocabulary items, selecting the substituted option. For the example stimulus item above, the child may choose the picture that shows Mommy pushing Daddy, substituting *pushing* for *kissing*.

Note that all reversible sentences are probable and the vocabulary demands are minimal for this procedure.

PASSING RESPONSE

The child responds correctly to the majority of items in each category (S-V, V-O, S-PP, S-V-O reversible sentences, S-V-PP reversible sentences, and V-O-PP reversible sentences).

<table>
<tr><td>FOR USE WITH
PROCEDURE:
3.7</td><td>◇</td><td>SCORE SHEET
Word Order
Comprehension</td></tr>
</table>

___

Instructions: For each stimulus item, record the number of the picture (1–4) to which the child points. Complete the pretest before proceeding with the test items.

___

Child's name: _____

Child's chronological age (years.months): _____

Date: _____

Pretest

A. Daddy _____
    Girl _____
    Boy _____
    Mommy _____

B. Crawling _____
    Hugging _____
    Kissing _____
    Climbing _____

C. Pouring _____
    Pushing _____
    Touching _____
    Dropping _____

D. In _____
    Blanket _____
    Cup _____
    On _____

E. Pitcher _____
    Water _____
    Doll _____
    Truck _____

Test

1. _____
2. _____
3. _____
4. _____
5. _____
6. _____
7. _____
8. _____

9. _____
10. _____
11. _____
12. _____
13. _____
14. _____
15. _____
16. _____

17. _____
18. _____
19. _____
20. _____
21. _____
22. _____
23. _____
24. _____

The Clinical Assessment of Language Comprehension
by Jon F. Miller and Rhea Paul   © 1995 Paul H. Brookes Publishing Co., Baltimore

<table>
<tr><td>FOR USE WITH PROCEDURE: 3.7</td></tr>
</table>

◇

INTERPRETATION FORM
Word Order
Comprehension

Instructions: This form is intended to be used with the score sheet for Procedure 3.7 (see p. 52). For each plate entry below, circle the child's response number. Total the columns as indicated. Upon completion, proceed with data analysis as described in Procedure 3.7.

Child's name: _____

Child's chronological age (years.months): _____

Date: _____

	Plate	Correct	Reversed	Unrelated	Substituted
S-V sentences	1	1	2	3	4
	2	4	1	2	3
	3	3	4	1	2
	4	2	3	4	1
Total S-V (1–4)					
V-O sentences	5	2	1	3	4
	6	4	3	1	2
	7	3	4	2	1
	8	1	2	4	3
Total V-O (5–8)					
S-PP sentences	9	2	4	1	3
	10	3	2	4	1
	11	1	3	2	4
	12	4	1	3	2
Total S-PP (9–12)					
Total two-element sentences (1–12)					
S-V-O sentences	13	4	2	3	1
	14	1	4	2	3
	15	3	1	4	2
	16	2	3	1	4
Total S-V-O (13–16)					
S-V-PP sentences	17	2	4	3	1
	18	4	2	1	3
	19	3	1	2	4
	20	1	3	4	2
Total S-V-PP (17–20)					
V-O-PP sentences	21	3	2	1	4
	22	2	1	4	3
	23	1	4	3	2
	24	4	3	2	1
Total V-O-PP (21–24)					
Total three-element sentences (13–24)					
Grand total (1–24)					

STIMULUS ITEMS
Word Order
Comprehension

Pretest

A. Daddy
   Girl
   Boy
   Mommy

B. Crawling
   Hugging
   Kissing
   Climbing

C. Pouring
   Pushing
   Touching
   Dropping

D. In
   Blanket
   Cup
   On

E. Pitcher
   Water
   Doll
   Truck

Test

Subject-Verb (S-V)

1. Mommy's kissing.
2. Daddy's kissing.
3. Daddy's hugging.
4. Mommy's hugging.

Verb-Object (V-O)

5. Pushing the girl.
6. Pushing the boy.
7. Touching the boy.
8. Touching the girl.

Subject-Prepositional Phrase (S-PP)

9. Doll on blanket.
10. Blanket on doll.
11. Cup in water.
12. Water in cup.

Subject-Verb-Object (S-V-O)

13. Daddy's kissing Mommy.
14. Mommy's kissing Daddy.
15. Mommy's hugging Daddy.
16. Daddy's hugging Mommy.

Subject-Verb-Prepositional Phrase (S-V-PP)

17. The boy climbs on Daddy.
18. Daddy climbs on the boy.
19. The girl crawls on Mommy.
20. Mommy crawls on the girl.

Verb-Object-Prepositional Phrase (V-O-PP)

21. Touching the water in the cup.
22. Touching the cup in the water.
23. Hugging the doll on the blanket.
24. Hugging the blanket on the doll.

The Clinical Assessment of Language Comprehension
by Jon F. Miller and Rhea Paul   © 1995 Paul H. Brookes Publishing Co., Baltimore

Daddy/Girl/Boy/Mommy

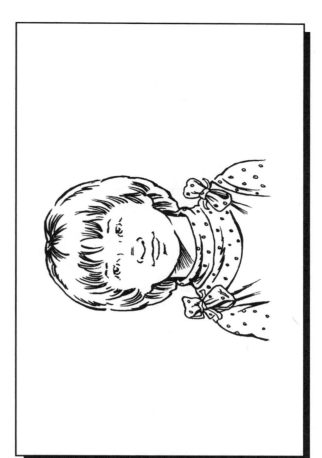
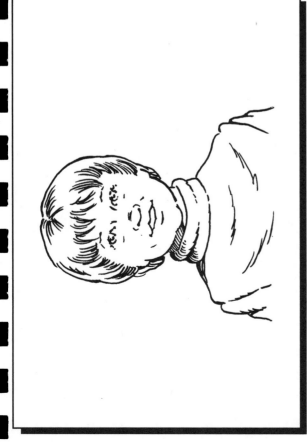

Crawling/Hugging/Kissing/Climbing

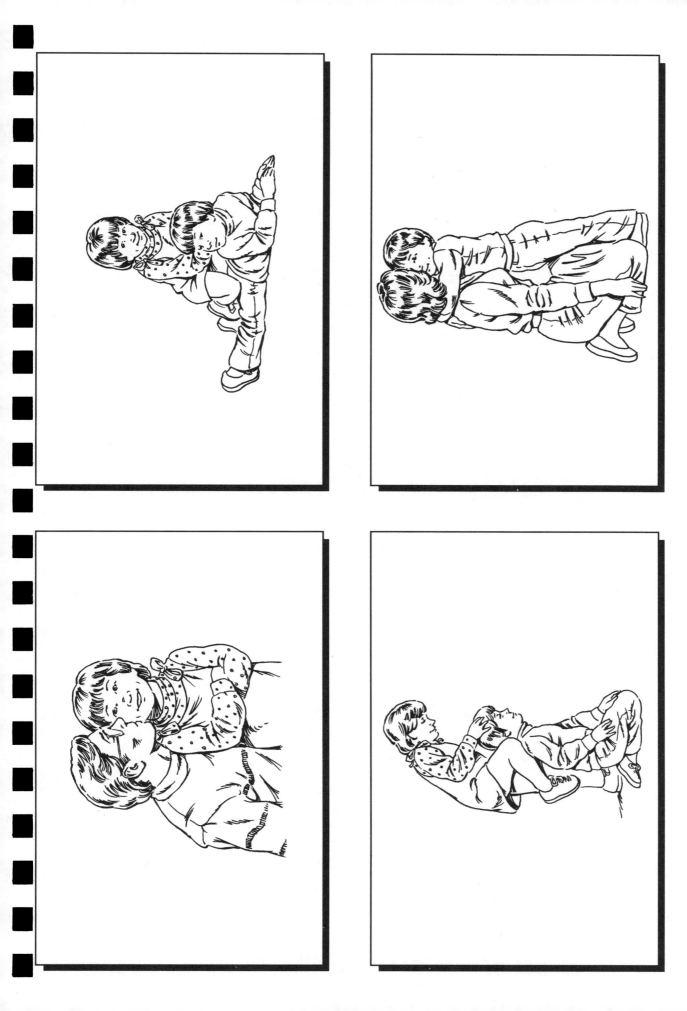

Pouring/Pushing/Touching/Dropping

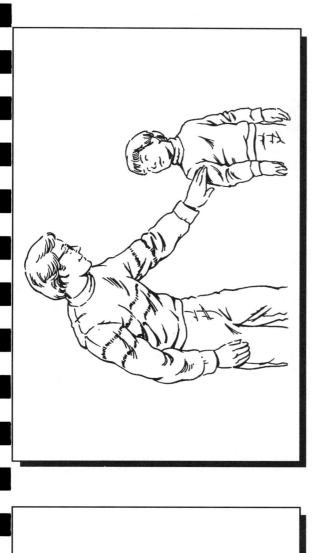

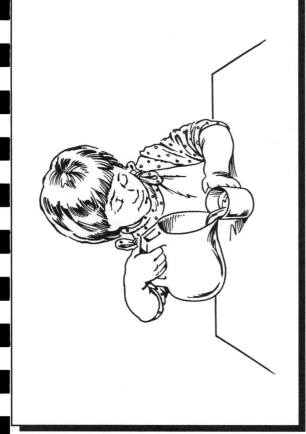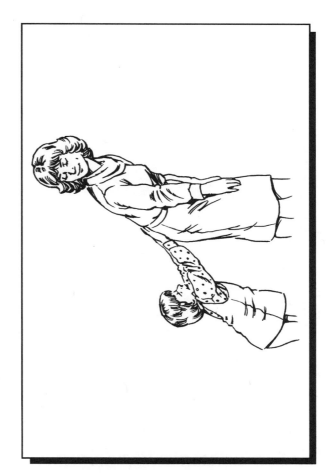

In/Blanket/Cup/On

In/Blanket/Cup/On

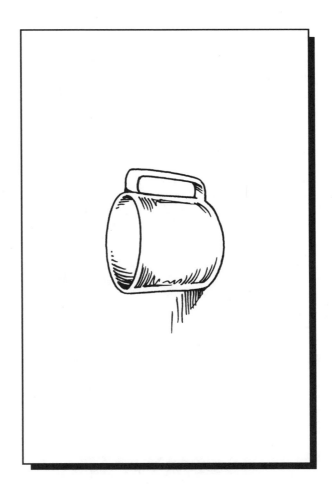

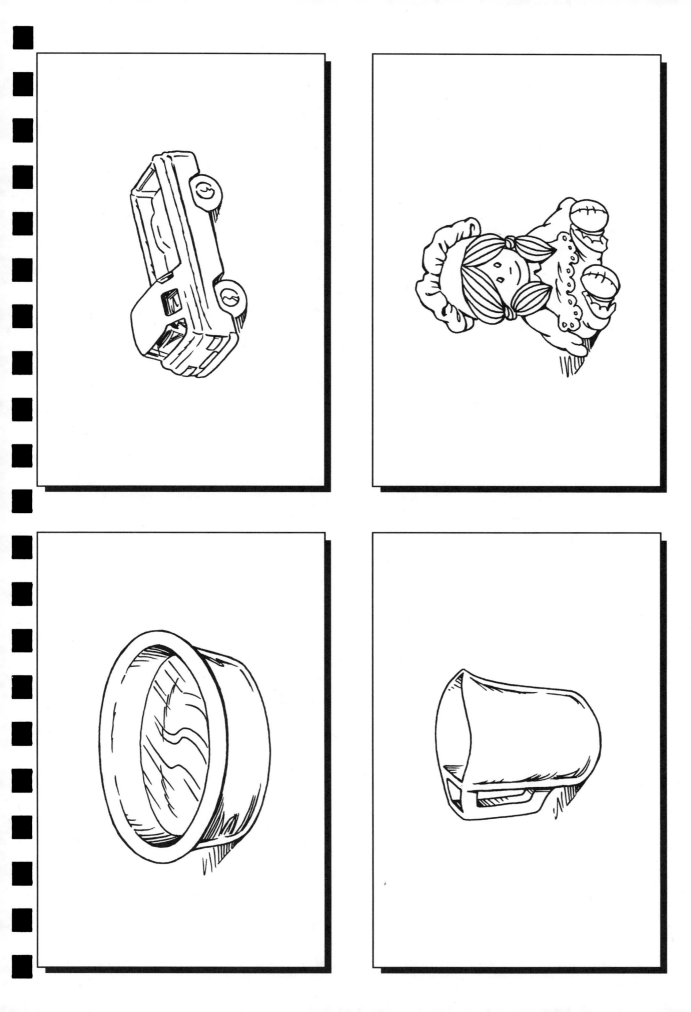

Mommy's kissing.

66   Mommy's kissing.

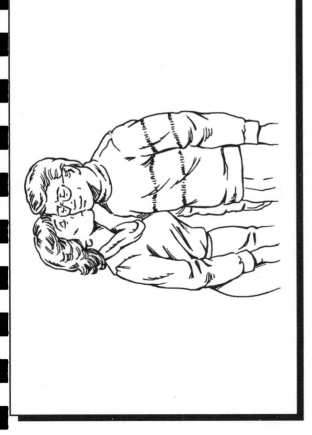

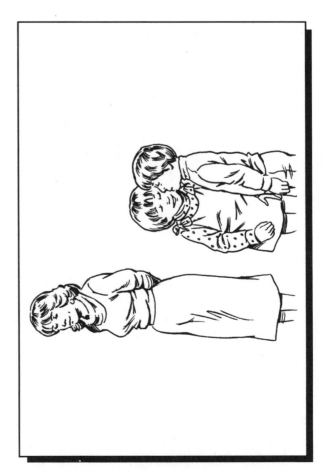

Daddy's kissing.

68   Daddy's kissing.

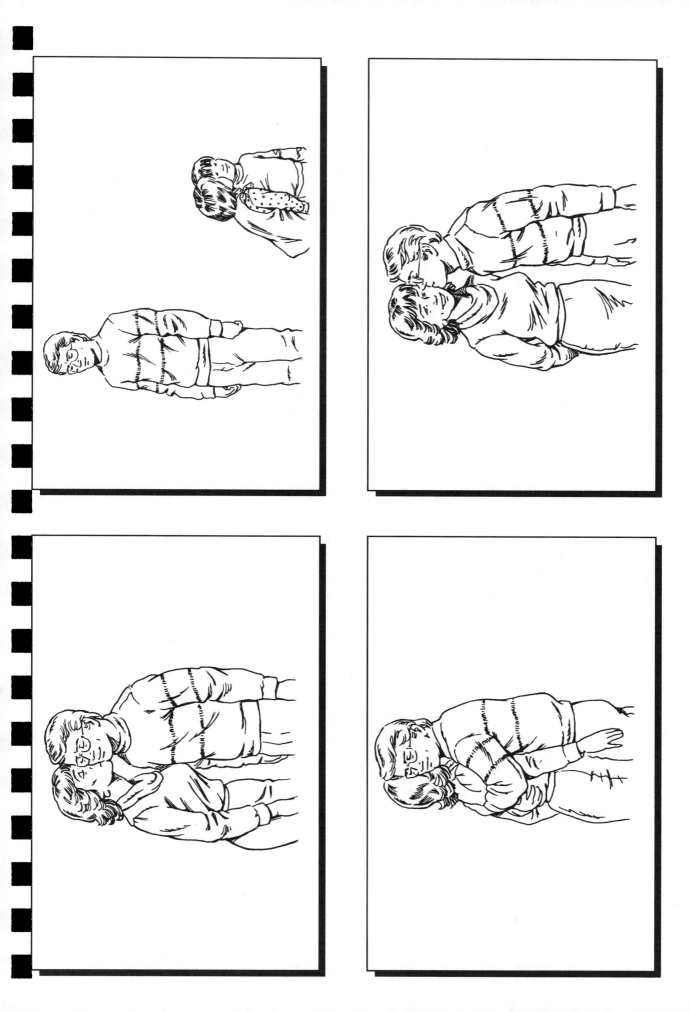

Daddy's hugging.

70   Daddy's hugging.

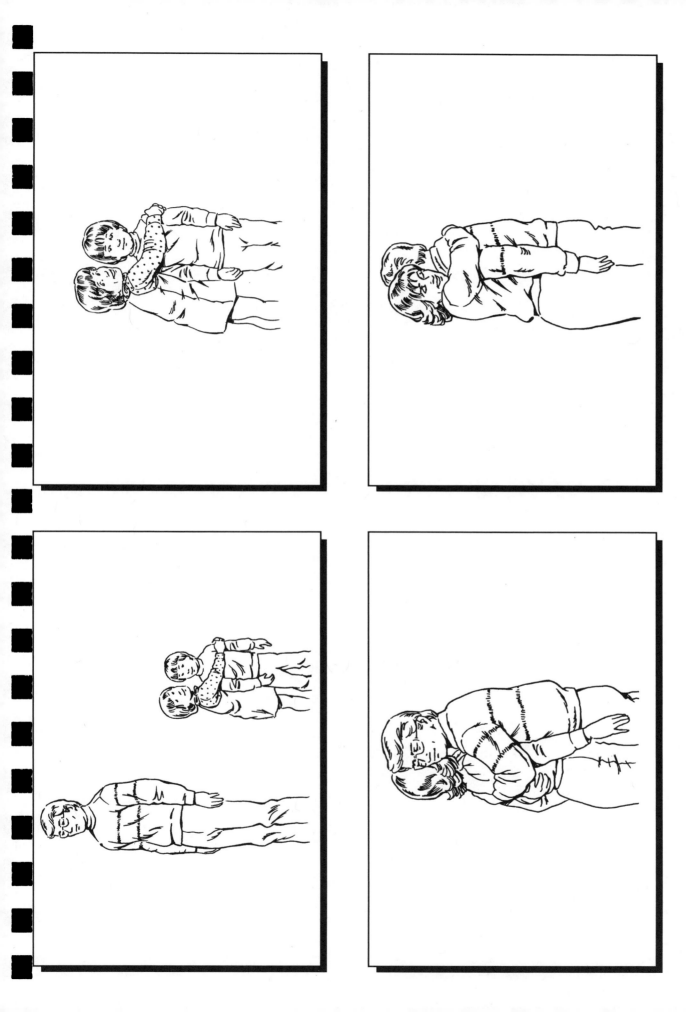

Mommy's hugging.

Mommy's hugging.

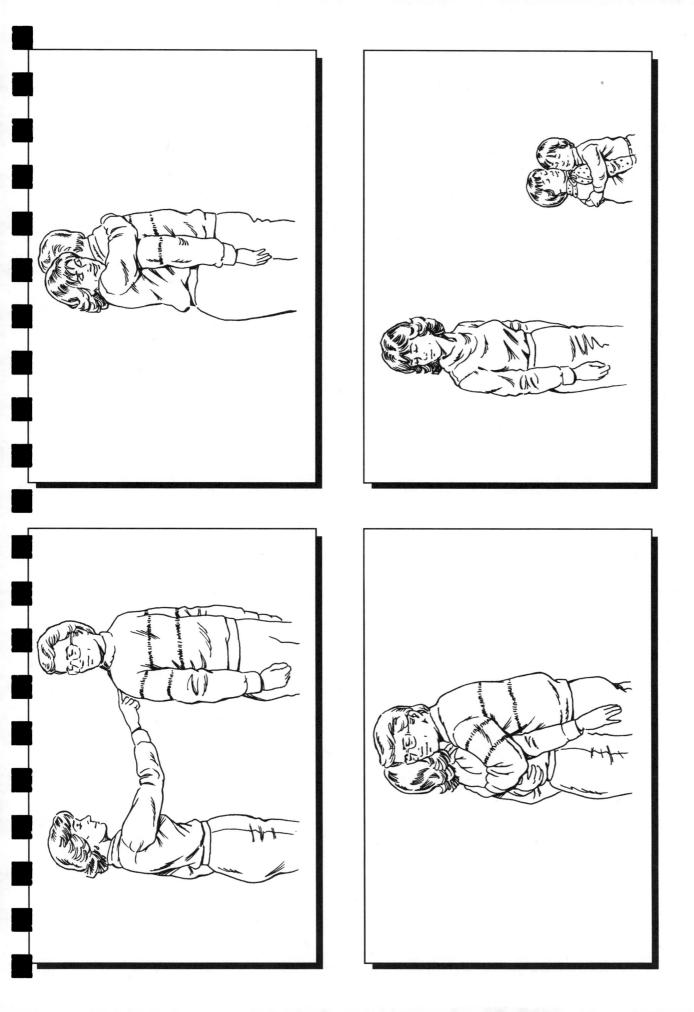

Pushing the girl.

Pushing the girl.

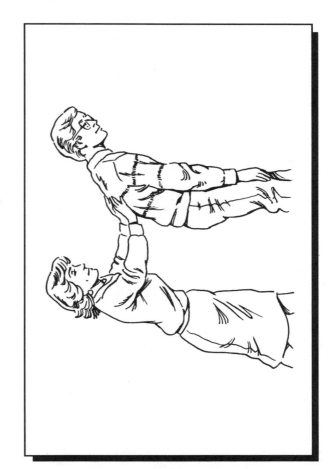

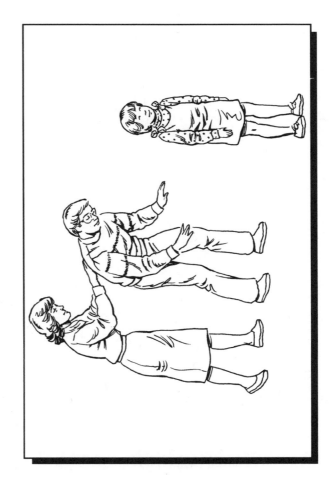

Pushing the boy.

76   Pushing the boy.

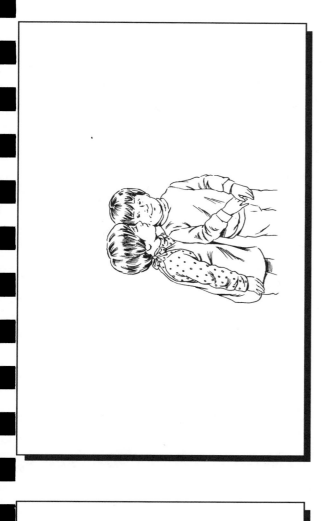

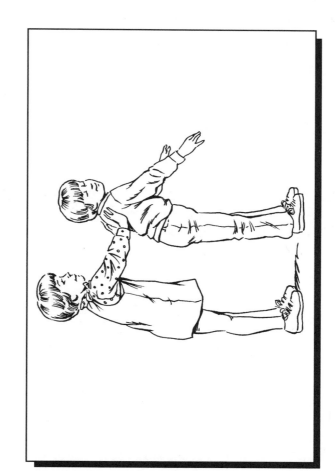

Touching the boy.

Touching the boy.

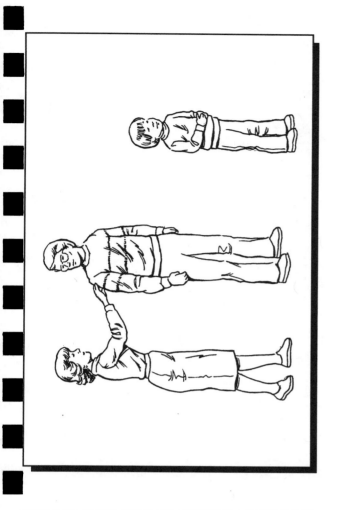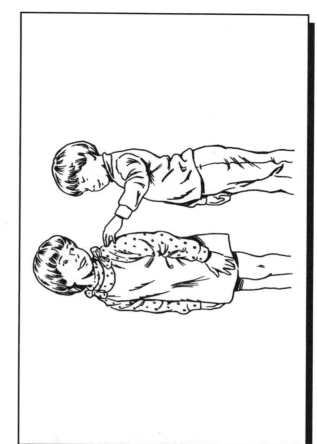

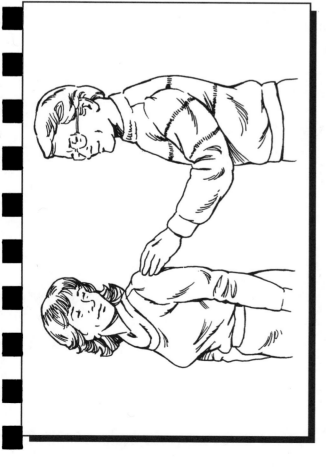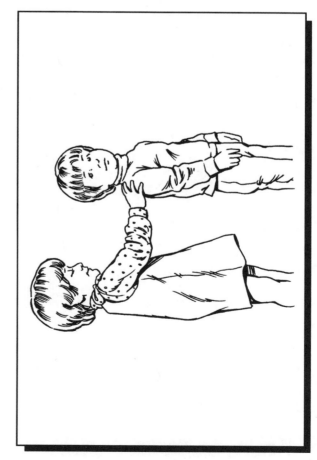

Touching the girl.

80   Touching the girl.

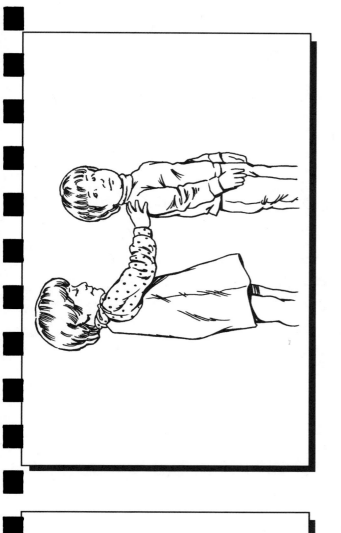

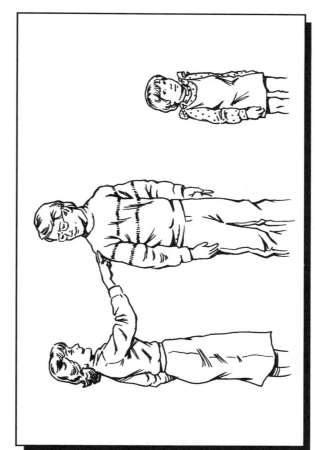

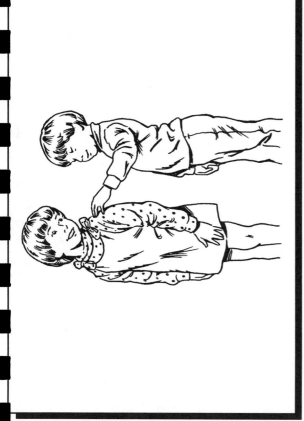

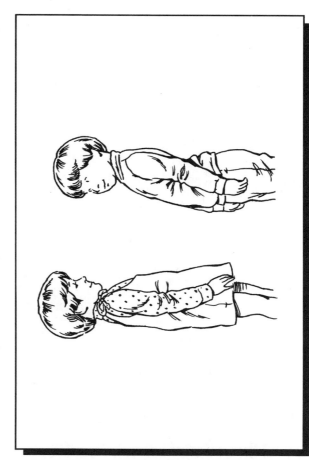

Doll on blanket.

Doll on blanket.

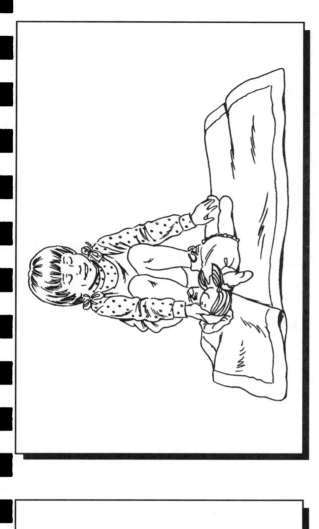

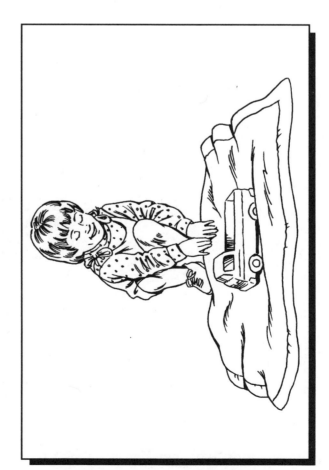

Blanket on doll.

Blanket on doll.

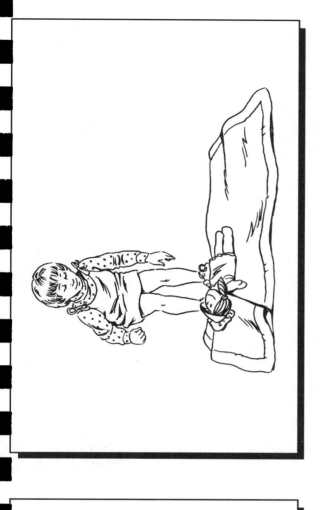

Cup in water.

Cup in water.

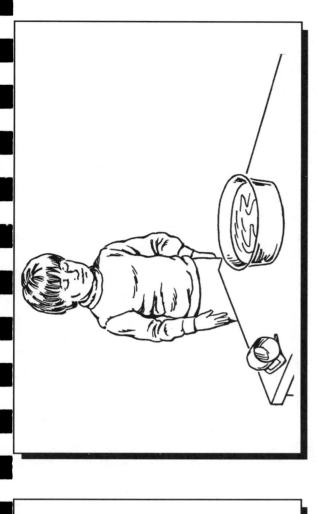

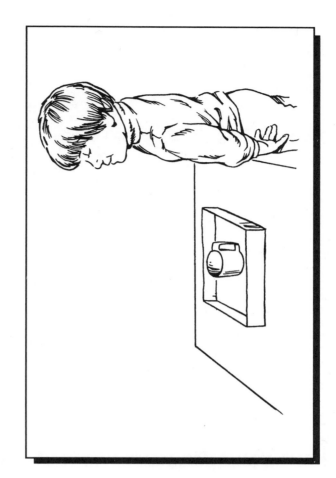

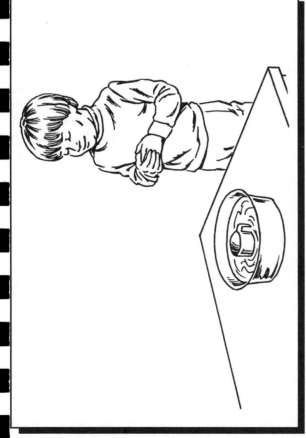

Water in cup.

Water in cup.

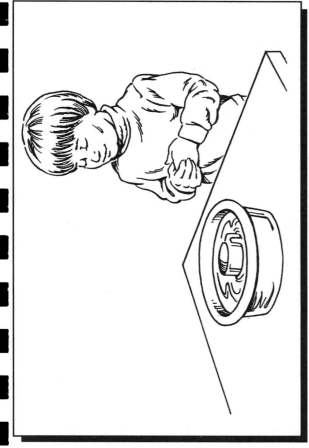

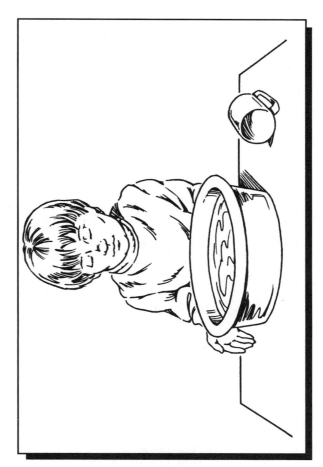

Daddy's kissing Mommy.

90   Daddy's kissing Mommy.

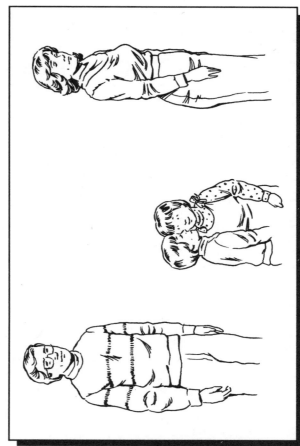

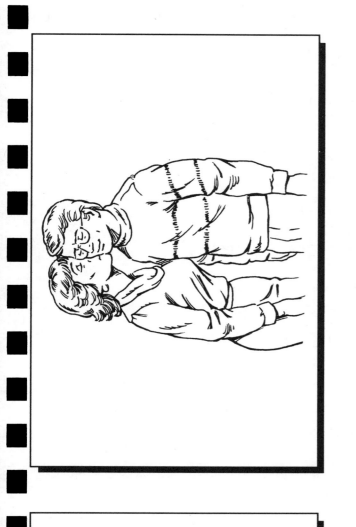

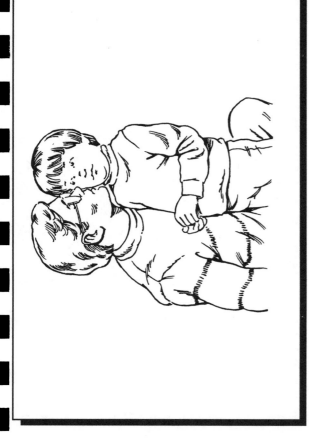

Mommy's kissing Daddy.

Mommy's kissing Daddy.

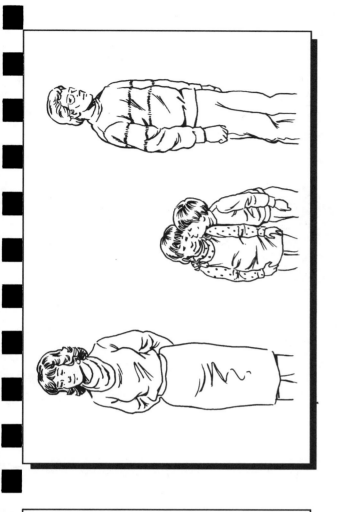

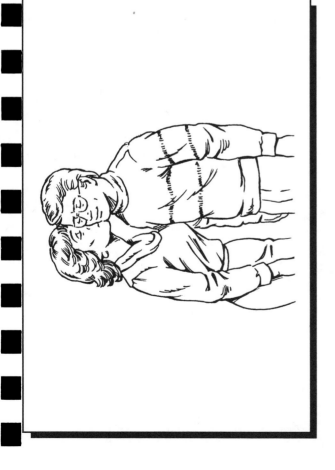

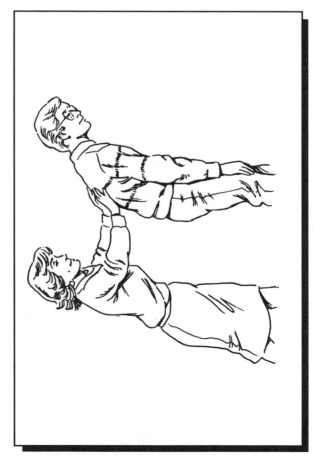

Mommy's hugging Daddy.

94   Mommy's hugging Daddy.

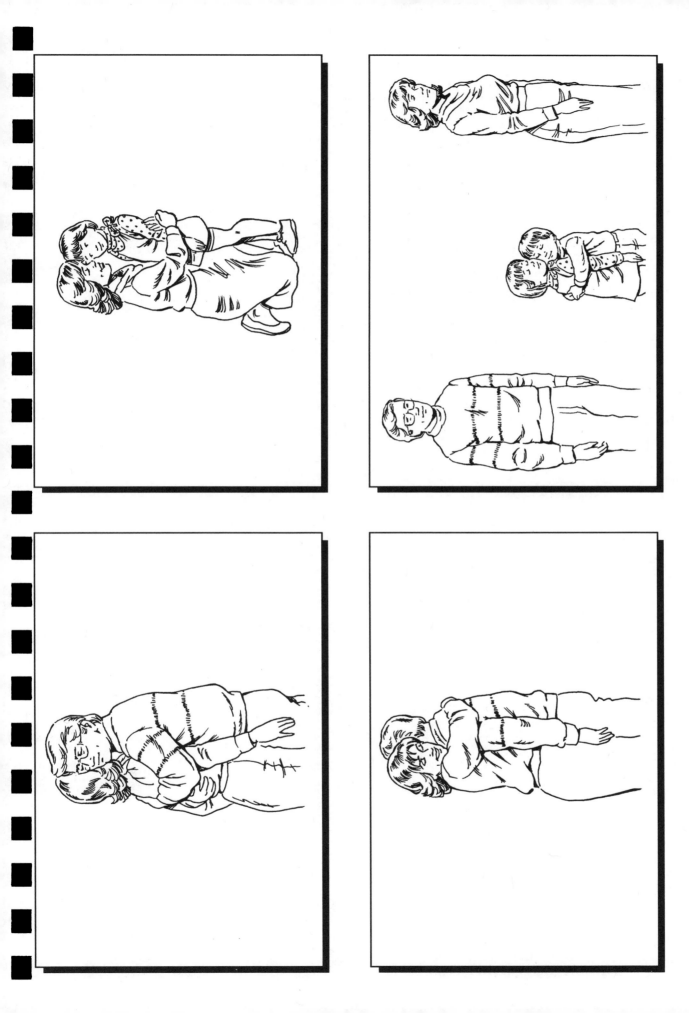

Daddy's hugging Mommy.

Daddy's hugging Mommy.

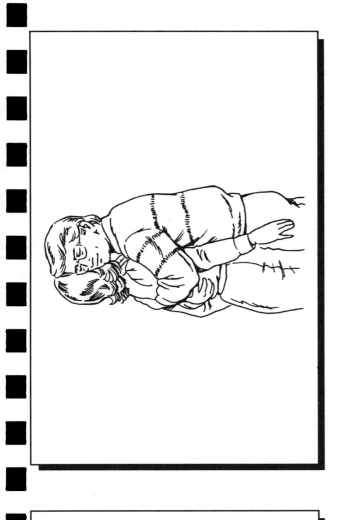

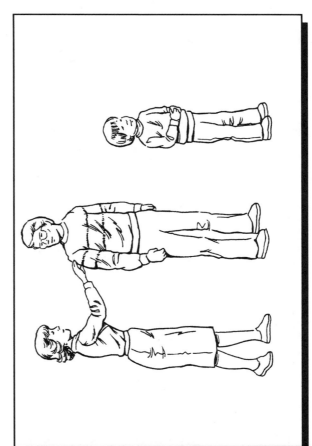

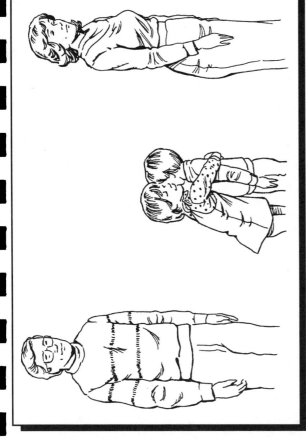

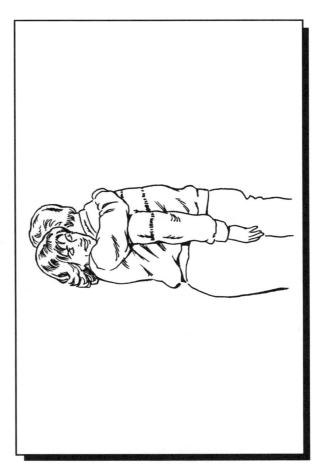

The boy climbs on Daddy.

The boy climbs on Daddy.

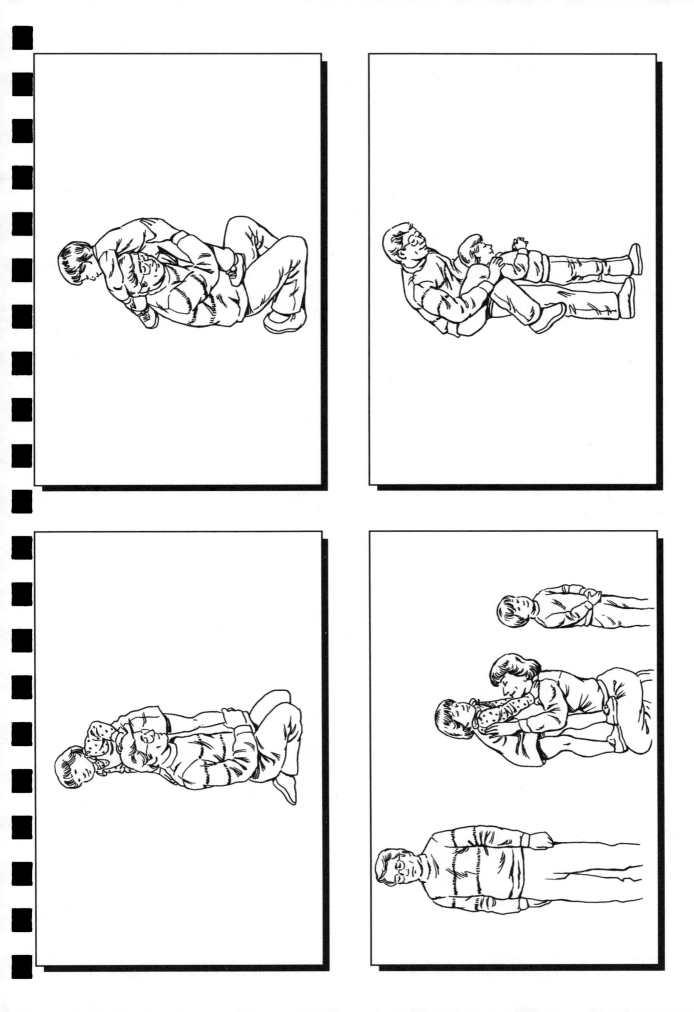

Daddy climbs on the boy.

Daddy climbs on the boy.

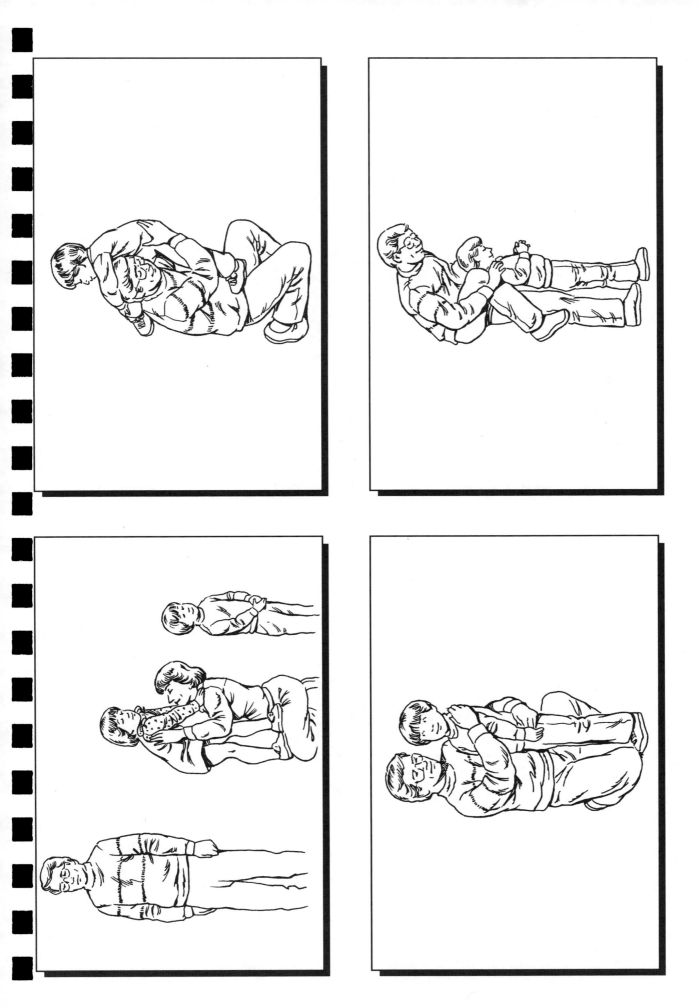

The girl crawls on Mommy.

The girl crawls on Mommy.

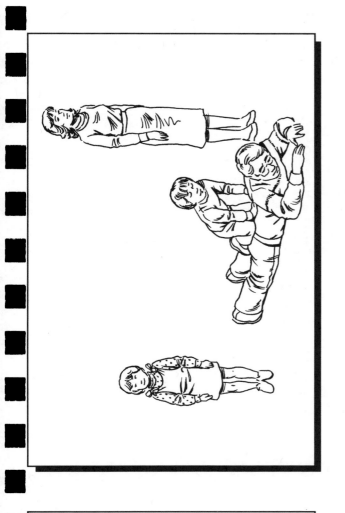

Mommy crawls on the girl.

Mommy crawls on the girl.

Touching the water in the cup.

Touching the water in the cup.

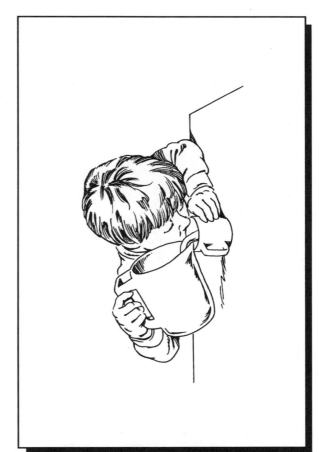

Touching the cup in the water.

Touching the cup in the water.

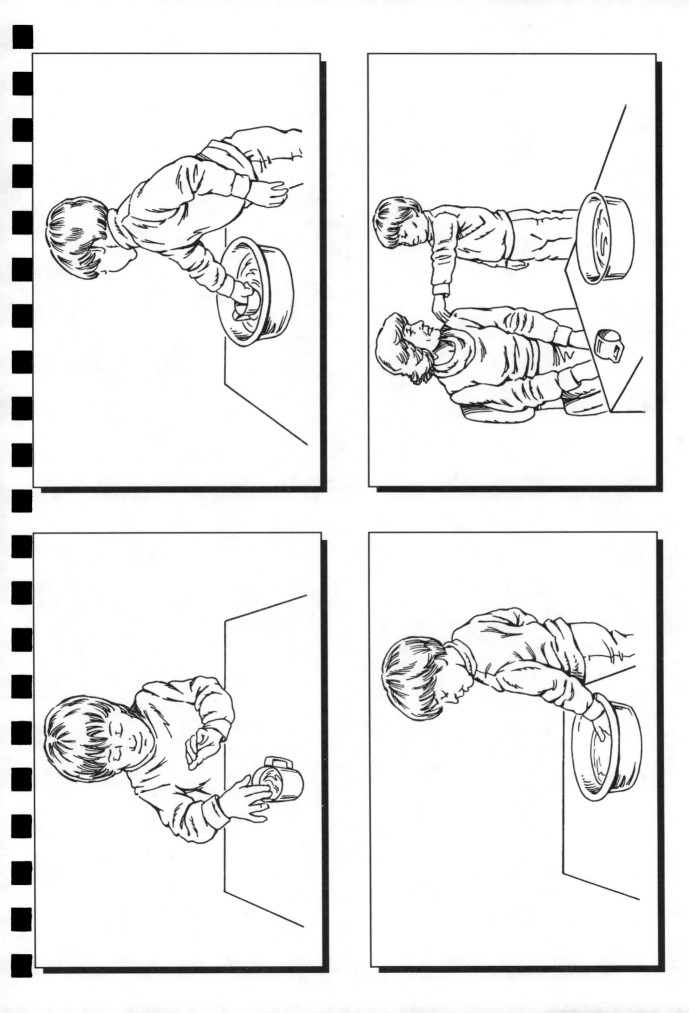

Hugging the doll on the blanket.

Hugging the doll on the blanket.

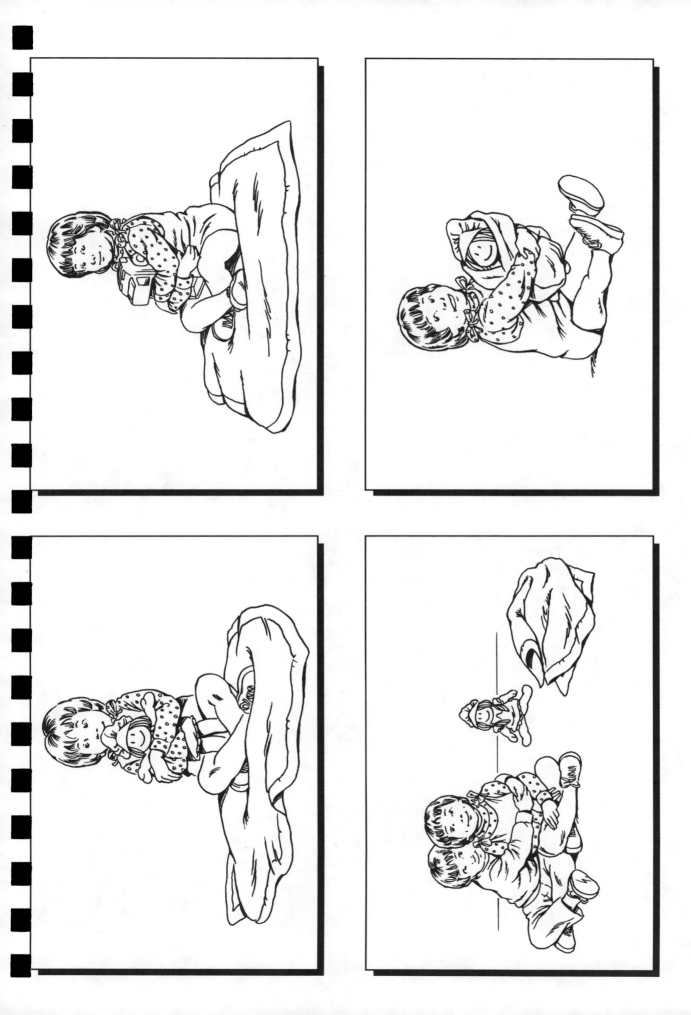

Hugging the blanket on the doll.

Hugging the blanket on the doll.

| PROCEDURE | Question Comprehension: |
| 3.8 ◇ | Conversational Format |

DEVELOPMENTAL LEVEL   24–60 months

LINGUISTIC LEVEL   Lexical/syntactic

LINGUISTIC STIMULI   Wh- question words and question forms listed on the score sheet on page 127

RESPONSE TYPE   Natural—answers

MATERIALS
- Pretend-play materials, storybooks, sequence cards, and puppets appropriate for the conversational context
- Tape recorder and cassettes (optional)

PROCEDURE
1. In the course of an ordinary conversation, ask questions that include the question words being tested. A variety of conversational contexts may be used, including:

   a. *Free play:* Ask a series of questions that are appropriate for the theme of the play. You may have to make sure that the toys selected allow for the needed question forms to be asked a number of times.

   b. *Storybooks:* You will have more control over the question forms to be asked because the questions can be preplanned around the events in the stories.

   c. *Snack time:* Ask the child about the food being eaten, home activities, how the child got to the evaluation setting, and so forth. This activity can be set up so that some questions are preplanned and others occur spontaneously from the child's interest.

   d. *Sequence cards:* Allow the child to answer questions about the story sequence the examiner has arranged. If the child is willing or capable, have him or her make up a story and then you ask questions about it.

   e. *Puppet play:* Puppets can be used to act out a story while the child watches. Give the child information about the action of the story, and then ask the child questions about the action.

2. Record responses on a score sheet like the one on page 127.

PASSING RESPONSE

Answers to questions are considered correct if they are semantically appropriate (i.e., a number answer is given to a "How many?" question) even if the answer is not true, such as:

Clinician: How many fingers do I have?

Child: Three.

Each question word should be tested several times and more than one correct response should be obtained before giving credit for comprehension of any question form.

RESPONSE STRATEGY

- "Supplying the missing information"

PROCEDURAL NOTES

- The score sheet on page 127 provides a developmental sequence for the order of acquisition of answers to questions in typically developing preschoolers. It is designed to serve as a score sheet for recording data on children's answers to questions.
- It is a good idea to tape record the question–answer session in order to have a record of the specific questions asked, the responses, and the preceding and following conversational context. This will provide the necessary data to interpret questionable responses where intervening variables, such as grammatical complexity of the question, may affect the child's response.
- It is imperative that you do not ask questions about information the child knows you already have. Asking questions about obvious information will result in the child refusing to play with such a "silly adult."

◇ # Question Comprehension: Structured Format

DEVELOPMENTAL LEVEL	24–60 months
LINGUISTIC LEVEL	Lexical/syntactic
LINGUISTIC STIMULI	Question words and question forms listed on the score sheet on page xxx
RESPONSE TYPE	Natural—answers

MATERIALS

Dependent upon scripts; for scripts used as examples here, use the following:

For Script 1:

- Mommy, Daddy, and dog dolls
- Dollhouse with furniture, colored blocks, toy cars and trucks

For Script 2:

- Two hand puppets ("Monster" and "Grunge"), stick, cookies, toy trucks, pebbles, box

PROCEDURE

1. Devise a story script that includes information about which the child will be questioned.
2. Write test questions into the script.
3. Develop a script score sheet.

Two example story scripts, complete with test questions and corresponding score sheets (see pp. 128–130 and pp. 131–132), are provided here. You may use these or develop your own. Another possibility is to use a storybook (e.g., *Peter Rabbit*) as the basis for the procedure. As you administer this procedure (using a script provided here, one of your own creation, or a storybook), remember that the answers to some questions, such as "How far?" and "How much?", might be difficult to elicit in free conversation; avoiding this problem is the purpose of this procedure.

4. Tell the story or enact the script, embedding questions throughout the process. The goal of this procedure is to test comprehension, rather than memory, so ask each question immediately following the sentence containing the information necessary for the answer; for example:

> "Peter Rabbit ate lots of Farmer's carrots. How much did
> Peter Rabbit eat?"

5. Record the child's responses on the script score sheet. Indicate whether the child gave a correct motor response, correct verbal response, incorrect response, or no response. If the child tends to give motor rather than verbal responses, encourage him or her to speak. For example, you might say, "Please *tell* me the answer. I want to hear you say it."

6. Transfer the data on the script score sheet to a score sheet like the one on page 127. To facilitate data interpretation, record both correct motor and verbal responses as accurate responses.

7. Examine the question words the child consistently interpreted correctly and incorrectly. Target forms consistently answered incorrectly for intervention.

PASSING RESPONSE

Credit is given for semantically appropriate answers whether or not they are accurate according to the script. For example, if the child answers a "where" question with "away," rather than "home," this is scored as correct even though it is not strictly true according to the script. Remember that you are testing understanding of the question words only.

This format also allows for nonverbal responses. Pointing to the appropriate character or place may be credited as a correct answer. More than one correct response should be elicited for each question form.

RESPONSE STRATEGY

• "Supplying the missing information"

To determine if this strategy is being used, examine the forms that were answered incorrectly consistently—for example, did the child consistently answer "how" questions as "what" questions?

PROCEDURE 3.10 ◇ Understanding of Preparatory and Sincerity Conditions for Speech Acts

DEVELOPMENTAL LEVEL

36–84 months

LINGUISTIC LEVEL

Discourse

LINGUISTIC STIMULI

Requests, some of which violate typical preparatory and sincerity conditions (e.g., "Please give me that. I don't want it."; "Put the dolls in this box. They belong in this bag.")

RESPONSE TYPE

Contrived—judgment

MATERIALS

• Puppets and assorted toys

PROCEDURE

1. Explain to the child that the puppet would like to play with him or her.
2. Tell the child that sometimes the puppet may ask for things and sometimes the puppet asks "right," and sometimes he asks "funny."
3. Engage the child in play and make a series of requests in the context of the play.
4. Intersperse felicitous and infelicitous forms, such as the following:

Felicitous	Infelicitous
Can I have that? I need it.	Can I have that? I don't really need it.
Come here. I want to show you something.	Come here. There's nothing over here.
Stop that! It hurts.	Stop that! I like it.
Put the car here. It goes in the garage.	Put the car here. It belongs over there.
Help me with this. I can't do it.	Help me with this. I can do it myself.

5. Record the child's responses on a score sheet like the one on page 133.

PASSING RESPONSE

The child gives some indication of realizing the infelicity of the anomalous requests by refusing to comply, saying "that's silly." The child who has a solid knowledge of the felicity conditions for requests should recognize more than half of the infelicitous requests.

| PROCEDURE 3.11 | ◇ | # Recognizing Polite Requests |

DEVELOPMENTAL LEVEL　　36–84 months

LINGUISTIC LEVEL　　Discourse

LINGUISTIC STIMULI　　Requests of varying levels of politeness

RESPONSE TYPE　　Contrived—judgment

MATERIALS
- Puppets
- Pieces of candy

PROCEDURE

1. Explain to the child that the puppets would like to get some candy, and the child should only give candy to those who ask nicely. If the puppet does not ask nicely, the child can tell the puppet to "ask nicer."

2. Have the puppet ask for the candy with requests of varying degrees of politeness, such as:

   Give me candy!
   I want candy.
   Can I have some candy?
   Would you give me some candy?

3. After each response, have the child decide whether the puppet asked nicely. If so, the child may give it candy. If not, the child should tell the puppet to "ask nicer."

4. Have the puppet ask for the candy again. Second requests should vary as to whether or not they are more polite than the first.

5. Have the child judge if the second request is nicer or not. (The child should also receive some candy at some point in the procedure.)

6. Using a score sheet like the one on page 134, record the child's judgment as nice or not nice. Indicate whether the child's judgment is correct or incorrect. Enter the second request given and the child's response to it (nicer or not nicer). Record whether the child's response is correct or incorrect.

PASSING RESPONSE　　If the child recognizes increments in politeness accurately more than 60% of the time, this skill can be seen as acquired.

119

| PROCEDURE | Responding to |
| 3.12 | ◇ Requests for Clarification |

DEVELOPMENTAL LEVEL   36–84 months

LINGUISTIC LEVEL   Discourse

LINGUISTIC STIMULI   Requests for clarification (e.g., What? A what?)

RESPONSE TYPE   Natural—answers to questions

MATERIALS
- Toys or picturebooks
- Tape recorder and cassettes

PROCEDURE
1. Engage the child in a conversation around a set of toys or a picture-book.
2. At appropriate points, interject "What?" or "A what?" as requests for clarification of the previous utterance.
3. Tape record conversation for later analysis.
4. Analyze the conversation. To do this, you can either transcribe the entire conversation from the cassette tape to document each request and response, or you may listen to the cassette tape and record the child's responses on a score sheet like the one on page 135. Transcription is more time consuming but provides exact data. Listening and recording responses is more efficient but provides more general data.

PASSING RESPONSE   By age 3, typically developing children distinguish between nonspecific requests for complete repetition of an entire utterance ("What?") and requests for specific constituents within the utterance ("A what?"). Correction responses include repeating the whole utterance in response to "What?" and supplying only the constituent requested in response to "A what?" Children over a developmental level of 3 years should respond appropriately to most requests for clarification.

PROCEDURE 3.13 ◇ Making Inferences in Discourse

DEVELOPMENTAL LEVEL	36–84 months
LINGUISTIC LEVEL	Discourse
LINGUISTIC STIMULI	Simple "stories" about a set of toys
RESPONSE TYPE	Contrived—object manipulation
MATERIALS	• Toys involved in the stories (e.g., toy rabbit, dishes)

PROCEDURE

1. Tell a series of simple stories such as the following:

   Story 1
   Rabbit's friends had a picnic for him.
   The picnic was in the woods.
   Where did Rabbit go?

   Story 2
   Mary was hungry.
   She went to McDonald's.
   What did she do there?

   Story 3
   The treasure was in the chest.
   The chest was buried under a great oak tree.
   Was the treasure buried?
   Where?

   Story 4
   Jim was cold.
   He went to his closet.
   What did he get?

2. Ask the child to answer an inference question about each.
3. If the child does not respond to a question, probe further using simple literal comprehension questions (e.g., "Who had a picnic for Rabbit?").
4. Record the child's responses on a score sheet like the one on page 136.

PASSING RESPONSE

The child makes an appropriate inference at least 50% of the time.

DIAGNOSTIC NOTE

If the child responds correctly to the literal questions but not the inference questions, there may be an inability to draw an inference. If the child does not respond or responds incorrectly to the literal questions, a more pervasive comprehension problem may be present.

<table>
<tr><td>FOR USE WITH PROCEDURE: 3.1</td></tr>
</table>

◇ SCORE SHEET
Assessing
Illocutionary Intent in Requests

Instructions: In the left column, record the adult's request. In the middle column, describe the child's responses. The scoring key below should be used to code the child's response to each adult request in the right column.

Child's name: _____

Child's chronological age (years.months): _____

Date: _____

Adult's request	Child's response	Score

Scoring key: + = Correct response
 − = Incorrect response
NR = No response
 IN = Inappropriate response

The Clinical Assessment of Language Comprehension
by Jon F. Miller and Rhea Paul © 1995 Paul H. Brookes Publishing Co., Baltimore

<table>
<tr><td rowspan="2">FOR USE WITH PROCEDURE: 3.2</td></tr>
</table>

FOR USE WITH
PROCEDURE:
3.2

◇ # SCORE SHEET
Assessing
Contingent Responding

Instructions: In the left column, tally the adult's utterance. Then put a check in one of the columns to the right to indicate whether the child produced a contingent (C) response, a noncontingent (NC) response, an imitative (I) response, or no response (NR). Compute the percentage of contingent and imitative responses and compare these figures to the data on the next page.

Child's name: _____

Child's chronological age (years.months): _____

Date: _____

Adult's utterance	Child's response			
	C	NC	I	NR

Scoring key: C = Contingent response
                NC = Noncontingent response
                  I = Imitative response
                NR = No response

The Clinical Assessment of Language Comprehension
by Jon F. Miller and Rhea Paul   © 1995 Paul H. Brookes Publishing Co., Baltimore

Computations:

Percentage of times child's response is contingent:

_____	Number of contingent child responses
÷ _____	Total number of adult's utterances
= _____	Percentage of contingent child responses

Percentage of times child's response is imitative:

_____	Number of imitative child responses
÷ _____	Total number of adult's utterances
= _____	Percent of imitative child responses

Average distribution of topic continuations in children's utterances

Average age (months)	Average MLU	Contingent responses (%)	Imitative responses (%)	Total contingent + imitative responses (%)
21	1.26	21	18	39
25	2.60	33	6	39
36	3.98	46	2	48
46	4.45	96	2	98

Source: Bloom, Rocissano, & Hood (1976).

<table>
<tr><td>FOR USE WITH PROCEDURE: 3.3</td></tr>
</table>

◇

SCORE SHEET
Assessing Comprehension of Two- and Three-Word Instructions with Toys as Agents

Instructions: In the left column, list the stimulus items to be administered by the adult. In the middle column, record the child's response using the scoring key below. In the right column, notes may be made about the child's response; for example, if in response to "horse eat" the child picks up the toy horse and flies it around the room, a note should be made that the child selected the correct agent.

Child's name: _____

Child's chronological age (years.months): _____

Date: _____

Adult's utterance	Child's response	Notes about child's response
horse eat		
cow drink		
doll kiss comb		
horse eat spoon		

Scoring key: + = Correct response
    – = Incorrect response
   NR = No response
   IN = Inappropriate response

The Clinical Assessment of Language Comprehension
by Jon F. Miller and Rhea Paul   © 1995 Paul H. Brookes Publishing Co., Baltimore

◇ SCORE SHEET
Assessing
Comprehension of Locatives

Instructions: For each locative word (e.g., *in*), record in the box corresponding to the trial a ✓ for a correct response, an X for an incorrect response, or NR for no response. If you choose to assess locatives with Procedure 3.4, use the Search Task grid to record responses. If you choose Procedure 3.5 or 3.6, use the Placement Task grid. (Only one of these procedures is needed to assess locative comprehension for any given child. Choose the procedure that best seems to address the child's abilities and interests.) If the child's response is incorrect, note the number of the preposition that indicates the child's response. For example, if in the Placement Task the child was told to place the object *beside* the mailbox and he or she placed it *in* the mailbox, record X1 in the box for that trial. Later, review these responses for patterns of response strategies. If there is no response, this should *not* be recorded as an incorrect response. Normative data are provided below for comparative purposes.

Child's name: _____

Child's chronological age (years.months): _____

Date: _____

	Search Task Trials									Placement Task Trials								
	1	2	3	4	5	6	7	8	9	1	2	3	4	5	6	7	8	9
1. In																		
2. On																		
3. Under																		
4. Behind																		
5. In front of																		
6. Beside																		

Percentage correct scores for two age groups on placement and search tasks for locatives

30 months

Locative	Placement	Search	Combined
In	87.5	83.3	85.4
On	62.5	58.3	60.4
Under	50.0	70.8	60.4
Behind	4.2	33.3	18.8
In front of	8.3	37.5	22.9
Beside	0.0	0.0	0.0

42 months

Locative	Placement	Search	Combined
In	100.0	100.0	100.0
On	95.8	100.0	97.9
Under	79.2	83.3	81.3
Behind	58.5	66.7	62.5
In front of	70.8	87.5	79.2
Beside	37.5	50.0	43.8

Source: Hodun (1975).

The Clinical Assessment of Language Comprehension
by Jon F. Miller and Rhea Paul   © 1995 Paul H. Brookes Publishing Co., Baltimore

FOR USE WITH PROCEDURES: 3.8   3.9

◇ **SCORE SHEET**
Assessing
Answers to Questions

Instructions: This form provides spaces to record responses for as many as four trials per question type entry. More trials may be used, if necessary, by photocopying this form. Fewer than four trials may be used, but a minimum of two is recommended. The scoring key below should be used to code the child's responses. If the child responds inappropriately (e.g., *IN* is entered for response), make notes about the child's response(s) in the right column. These notes will enable you to determine how the child is interpreting specific question types and which response strategies he or she is using. For example, a child who consistently answers "why" questions as "what" questions may be using a "supply the missing information" response strategy. Knowing this can be helpful in planning intervention.

Child's name: _____

Child's chronological age (years.months): _____

Date: _____

Question type	Age of mastery	Trials 1	2	3	4	Notes on child's response
Yes/no	2.0+					
What?	2.6+					
What (X) doing?	2.6+					
Where (place)?	2.6+					
Where (direction)?	2.6+					
Whose?	3.0+					
Who?	3.0+					
Why?	3.0+					
How many?	3.0+					
How?	3.6+					
How much?	4.0+					
How long (duration)?	4.0+					
How far?	4.0+					
How often?	4.6+					
When?	4.6+					
Based on Chapman (1973).						

Scoring key: + = (Semantically) correct response
           − = (Semantically) incorrect response
      NR = No response
      IN = Inappropriate response

The Clinical Assessment of Language Comprehension
by Jon F. Miller and Rhea Paul   © 1995 Paul H. Brookes Publishing Co., Baltimore

<table>
<tr><td>FOR USE WITH PROCEDURE: 3.9</td></tr>
</table>

SCRIPT SCORE SHEET
◇ Question Comprehension:
Structured Format

Instructions: This score sheet has been developed for the example script known as "The Car Story." For each question below, categorize and record the child's response in the correct column under scoring key. Remember that the child's response does not have to be strictly true to be recorded as correct. What is important is that the child give the correct type of answer.

Child's name: _____

Child's chronological age (years.months): _____

Date: _____

Script entry	Scoring key			
	Correct motor response	Correct verbal response	Incorrect response	No response
1. *Is this a dog?* (no) It's pretty. It's a car. Look it goes, Vroom! Vroom!				
2. It can go here. (on table) It goes fast. Bye-bye car. *Where is it going?* (Place in garage of dollhouse)				
3. Let's give Mommy a ride. Here she goes. *Who is in the car?* Bye-bye, Mommy.				
4. Give me the toy. (Clinician places Mommy doll in bed.) *Where is she?* Mommy is tired. Mommy is going to bed.				
5. *What is Mommy doing?* *(sleeping)* Sh. Be very quiet. Don't wake Mommy. Here comes Daddy.				

The Clinical Assessment of Language Comprehension
by Jon F. Miller and Rhea Paul   © 1995 Paul H. Brookes Publishing Co., Baltimore

Script entry	Scoring key			
	Correct motor response	Correct verbal response	Incorrect response	No response
6. Daddy wants supper. Let's find something to eat. *Where is Daddy going?* (Clinician moves Daddy doll toward kitchen.) Sit down here, Daddy.				
7. Daddy's finished eating. That was good. *Who is eating?* Let's go for a walk.				
8. Daddy has a doggie. Here's the doggie. *Whose doggie?* The doggie is tired.				
9. Here is the ball. Let's play ball. It's red. *What is it?*				
10. Here comes doggie. Doggie says bow-wow. Doggie has two friends. *How many friends?*				
11. Look at Daddy (Clinician moves Daddy doll in walking fashion.) *What is Daddy doing?* Hurry up, Daddy. Sit down.				
12. *Who sits down?* Daddy's in the chair. Daddy reads the book Here comes Mommy.				

The Clinical Assessment of Language Comprehension
by Jon F. Miller and Rhea Paul   © 1995 Paul H. Brookes Publishing Co., Baltimore

Script entry	Scoring key			
	Correct motor response	Correct verbal response	Incorrect response	No response
13. Mommy says Hi. *Whose book?* It's a storybook.				
14. *Whose is it?* (Point to child's shoe) See my watch. My watch goes tick, tick. It's round.				
15. I like toys. *Is Mommy here?* Stand up. Sit down.				
16. Here are the blocks. (Clinician dumps blocks on table.) Oh look. *How many?* Let's put the key away.				
17. Here is something It's red. It's square. *Is it a block?*				
18. *How many?* (Clinician adds blocks.) I'll put one here and here (builds tower) Push them down.				
19. Look at this. (Clinician gets a truck.) See it go. *What is this?* (truck) Vroom. Vroom.				
20. Put the blocks in the truck. Watch the truck. (Clinician moves the truck.) *What is it doing?* It can go fast.				

The Clinical Assessment of Language Comprehension
by Jon F. Miller and Rhea Paul   © 1995 Paul H. Brookes Publishing Co., Baltimore

<table>
<tr><td>FOR USE WITH PROCEDURE: 3.9</td></tr>
</table>

◇ **SCRIPT SCORE SHEET**
Question Comprehension:
Structured Format

Instructions: This score sheet has been developed for the example script known as " The Cookie Monster Story." For each question posed to the child, record the child's response verbatim in the third column.

Child's name: _____

Child's chronological age (years.months): _____

Date: _____

Action of puppets	Question to child	Child's response
Grunge hits Cookie Monster with a stick.	What is Grunge doing?	
Grunge hits Cookie Monster with a stick and says "I want your cookies."	How is Grunge hitting Cookie Monster?	
Grunge alternately hits Cookie Monster and Cookie Monster's cookies. Cookie Monster alternately cries "Ouch" when hit and "Oh, my poor cookies" when they are being hit. Narrator: Oh, no! Grunge is still *hitting*. Boy is he mean.	Why is Grunge hitting Cookie Monster?	
Grunge alternately punches Cookie Monster and throws rocks at him. Cookie Monster alternately cries "Ouch, mean Grunge" and "Ouch, Ooooo those rocks."	Who is hitting Cookie Monster?	
	What is hitting Cookie Monster?	

The Clinical Assessment of Language Comprehension
by Jon F. Miller and Rhea Paul   © 1995 Paul H. Brookes Publishing Co., Baltimore

Action of puppets	Question to child	Child's response
Cookie Monster retreats and hides under a box.	Where is Cookie Monster hiding?	
	Why is Cookie Monster hiding?	
Cookie Monster comes out of hiding and grabs the stick and starts hitting Grunge.	What is Cookie Monster doing?	
Cookie Monster hits Grunge with a stick, simultaneously saying, "I want my cookies back."	How is Cookie Monster hitting Grunge?	
	Why is Cookie Monster hitting Grunge?	
Cookie Monster alternately hits Grunge and Grunge's toy car. Grunge alternately cries "Ouch" when hit and "Oh, my poor car" when it is hit. Narrator: "Cookie Monster is hitting now."	Who is Cookie Monster hitting?	
	What is Cookie Monster hitting?	
Cookie Monster alternately hits Grunge and throws rocks at him. Grunge alternately cries "Ouch, mean Cookie Monster" and "Ouch, Ooooo those rocks."	Who is hitting Grunge?	
	What is hitting Grunge?	
Grunge retreats and hides under a box.	Why is Grunge hiding?	
Cookie Monster gets back his cookies.	Where is Grunge hiding?	

The Clinical Assessment of Language Comprehension
by Jon F. Miller and Rhea Paul   © 1995 Paul H. Brookes Publishing Co., Baltimore

<table>
<tr><td>FOR USE WITH PROCEDURE: 3.10</td></tr>
</table>

◇ # SCORE SHEET
Understanding of Preparatory and Sincerity Conditions for Speech Acts

Instructions: For each stimulus item, record the child's response in the third column. Then, mark in the fourth column whether the child's response is correct (✔), incorrect (X), or if no response (NR) is given. In the final column, observations may be recorded. These may include a questioning facial expression accompanying no response, which might indicate partial comprehension. Such indications could suggest speech acts that would be good first targets for intervention planning because the child has partial knowledge about them.

Child's name: _____

Child's chronological age (years.months): _____

Date: _____

Stimulus item	Correct response	Child's response	Correct?	Comments
Can I have that? I need it.	Felicitous			
Come here. I want to show you something.	Felicitous			
Can I have that? I don't really need it.	Infelicitous			
	Infelicitous			
	Felicitous			
	Felicitous			
	Infelicitous			
	Felicitous			
	Infelicitous			
	Infelicitous			

<table>
<tr><td>FOR USE WITH PROCEDURE: 3.11</td><td>◇</td><td>**SCORE SHEET**
Recognizing
Polite Requests</td></tr>
</table>

Instructions: In the first column, record the adult's first request. In the second column, record the child's response of "nice" or "not nice." Then indicate whether the child's response is correct (✔), incorrect (X), or if no response (NR) is given. For each incorrect response, make a second request of the child and record it in the column labeled as such. Mark the child's judgment and whether it is correct (✔), incorrect (X), or if no response (NR) is given.

Child's name: _____

Child's chronological age (years.months): _____

Date: _____

First request	Child's judgment	Correct?	Second request	Child's judgment	Correct?
Give me candy!					
I want candy.					
Can I have some candy?					
Would you give me some candy?					

The Clinical Assessment of Language Comprehension
by Jon F. Miller and Rhea Paul © 1995 Paul H. Brookes Publishing Co., Baltimore

<table>
<tr><td>FOR USE WITH
PROCEDURE:
3.12</td></tr>
</table>

FOR USE WITH PROCEDURE: 3.12

SCORE SHEET
Responding to
Requests for Clarification

Transcription Instructions: Record the child's preclarification-request statement in the first column (e.g., "I have a new truck"). In the second column, code your request for clarification as general (G) if you asked "What?" or specific (S) if you asked "A what?" In the third column, write the child's response to your question.

Instructions for On-Line Recording: Leave the first column blank. Record G or S in the second column as instructed above, and write the child's response in the third column.

Child's name: _____

Child's chronological age (years.months): _____

Date: _____

Child's statement	Adult's request	Child's response

The Clinical Assessment of Language Comprehension
by Jon F. Miller and Rhea Paul   © 1995 Paul H. Brookes Publishing Co., Baltimore

<table>
<tr>
<td>
FOR USE WITH
PROCEDURE:
3.13
</td>
<td>◇</td>
<td>
SCORE SHEET
Making Inferences in Discourse
</td>
</tr>
</table>

Instructions: In the second column, record the child's response to each question. In the third column, indicate whether the child's response was correct (✓) or incorrect (X). If the child gave no response (NR), probe by asking some simple literal comprehension questions (e.g., "Who had a picnic for Rabbit?"). If the child responds correctly to these literal questions, the NR entries can be interpreted as an inability to draw an inference. If the child does not respond or responds incorrectly to the literal questions, a more pervasive comprehension problem may be present.

Child's name: _____

Child's chronological age (years.months): _____

Date: _____

Questions	Child's response	Inference correct?
Story 1		
Question 1		
Question 2		
Question 3		
Story 2		
Question 1		
Question 2		
Question 3		
Story 3		
Question 1		
Question 2		
Question 3		
Story 4		
Question 1		
Question 2		
Question 3		
Story 5		
Question 1		
Question 2		
Question 3		
Story 6		
Question 1		
Question 2		
Question 3		

Scoring key: ✓ = Correct response
               X = Incorrect response
           NR = No response

The Clinical Assessment of Language Comprehension
by Jon F. Miller and Rhea Paul © 1995 Paul H. Brookes Publishing Co., Baltimore

4 ◇ Assessing Comprehension in the Language for Learning Stage

Developmental level: 5–10 years
Language level: Brown's stages V+; MLU 4.5 and up
Production milestones: Vocabulary is large (greater than 5,000 words). Basic syntax in simple sentences has been acquired; few grammatical errors are heard in speech. Some complex sentences (about 20% of utterances in speech samples from typically developing children [Paul 1981]) are used. Most morphological markers are used consistently, although a few errors (e.g., overgeneralization of past tense) may persist. Most phonological simplification processes have been eliminated; one or two may remain. Distortions of a few sounds may also be present. Speech is intelligible.

The third period of language development is the "language for learning," or L4L, stage of acquisition, so named because of the close connection between language skills and success in school during middle childhood. During this time, children do increasing amounts of their learning through the medium of language rather than through direct experience. In fact, much of the learning that goes on in middle childhood takes place through reading rather than through oral language (Dickinson, Wolf, & Stotsky, 1993). Not only new information but also new vocabulary and exposure to increasingly complex and "literate" styles of language are gained primarily through reading or through formal, decontextualized oral language (e.g., lectures) during this period (Westby, 1991). Because of these connections between language competence and the ability to acquire the information needed for academic success, the label for this stage emphasizes the interactions between language and learning. In addition, because of the great reliance on understanding so many new forms and discourse functions of language in order for learning to proceed, comprehension skills become particularly pivotal during this period.

TESTING OPTIONS IN THE L4L STAGE

When children reach the developmental level of 5 years or more, they are usually ready for the more structured standardized assessment procedures. These procedures offer the advantage of normative data that enable us to compare an individual child's performance with that of a large group of similar children on the same items presented in exactly the same manner. Clearly, where the use of such procedures is possible, confidence in the decision as to whether or not the child has a compre-

137

hension problem is improved. However, the child must meet the requirements specified by the test in order for the results to be interpreted correctly. Children with sensory or motor disorders may be unable to provide the types of responses demanded by standardized testing. Children with significant cognitive limitations are different in important ways from the norming population, who will be much younger than the child when they take the test. Lahey (1990) points out the difficulties of using formal tests normed for children of different chronological ages with older children who have decreased cognitive levels. And, as discussed previously, formal tests may not sample all of the structures and functions, particularly discourse functions, that we would like to assess. For these reasons, informal comprehension testing can be important during the L4L stage, even after a standardized test has been given to establish that a child's comprehension skills are different from those of other children. Of course, all of the procedures in this chapter must be administered with the same care for stimulus description and interpretation as the informal procedures in Chapters 2 and 3.

In addition to the fully nonstandardized procedures provided in this chapter, one instrument that straddles the border between formal and informal measures should be mentioned. The *Miller–Yoder (M–Y) Test of Language Comprehension* (Miller & Yoder, 1984) is a picture-pointing procedure that samples a variety of syntactic and morphological forms important for functioning in the late preschool and early school-age period. Each structure evaluated on the M–Y is tested in two pairs of stimulus sentences, with each pair containing one sentence representing the target structure and one sentence with the contrasting unmarked form (e.g., marbles/marble, is/is not). The child must respond correctly to both sentences to be credited for the pair and to both pairs to be credited for the structure. This procedure requires the child to demonstrate comprehension of the target structure as contrasted with the exact utterance without the contrasting form (e.g., The girl is running/The girl is not running). Furthermore, the opportunity for getting credit by guessing is reduced from 1 chance in 4 to 1 chance in 16. All items on the M–Y are designed with sentence length and vocabulary controlled so that the clinician can feel confident that the form being tested in each pair is the only variable that will affect the child's performance. Because each item tests a single grammatical form, item analysis can be used to identify specific comprehension problems and target them for intervention.

Normative data on the production of the forms tested on the M–Y are available and can be used to compare performance with that of peers. The real strength of the M–Y, though, is its capacity for adaptation as a criterion-referenced, rather than norm-referenced, procedure. Using it this way, decisions about comprehension–production gaps can be made by looking at the child's production in free speech and contrasting it with performance on same forms in the receptive mode on the M–Y. For example, suppose a child produces *in* and *on* correctly in free speech but does not use any other prepositions spontaneously. Comprehension of a range of locative prepositions could be assessed using the M–Y, and it could be determined whether receptive locative vocabulary is larger than that used in spontaneous speech. In addition, administration of the M–Y can be adapted to an individual child's disabilities. To do this, items can be given in the standard manner, then adapted, one variable at a time, in order to look for changes in performance. For example, although the instructions on the M–Y caution the clinician not to stress the form being tested, when giving the M–Y to a child with a hearing impairment, the clinician may want to alter intonation on these forms to ensure that they are received by the child. Care must be exercised in using the normative data for interpretation under these circumstances. Responses can be interpreted from a criterion-referenced point of view, though, noting the range of forms the child understood and the testing conditions. Again, this information is helpful in looking at gaps between comprehension and production, identifying targets for intervention, and evaluating progress in a treatment program. If the goal is to determine initially whether or not a child has a significant comprehension problem, a more standardized administration procedure will be necessary.

In the next part of this chapter, several specific procedures for assessing comprehension in the L4L stage are presented. The main change in the procedures in this chapter, relative to earlier chapters, is an increased reliance on judgment tasks, which are easy to administer and developmentally appropriate for this level. A second difference is that in the L4L stage, many aspects of literal semantic/syntactic comprehension can be assessed using standardized methods. As a result, the procedures in this chapter do not usually assess literal comprehension of so broad a range of semantic and syntactic forms. Instead, nonstandardized assessment will generally be used to evaluate discourse-level skills and to focus on a few specific forms that need further study to follow up standardized testing, or that are especially important for classroom success.

JUDGMENT TASKS

Judgment tasks have been used by a variety of investigators (e.g., de Villiers & de Villiers, 1973; James & Miller, 1973; Paul, 1985) to examine children's linguistic competence. They have the advantage of allowing the clinician to look at comprehension of sentences that may be difficult to depict or represent with objects. But as Table 1.4 showed, children may not perform appropriately on judgment tasks until some time after they have passed the same item on a picture-pointing or object manipulation task. Judgment tasks should be interpreted with care, then, because they seem to involve some higher-level processes than do the earlier developing responses. Failure to pass a judgment task for a particular structure may not mean that the child does not comprehend that structure. For some forms of interest, though (e.g., those containing items not easily pictured, those that refer to concepts rather than objects), judgment tasks may be the only method of assessment available (see Procedure 4.4, for example).

Several variations on the judgment task have been used in studying language acquisition. De Villiers and de Villiers (1973) present a puppet who "has trouble talking" and ask children simply to say when it says "something silly." Another method used by James and Miller (1973) and Paul (1985) presents the child with two pictures—one of an "OK lady" and one of a bizarre-looking "silly lady." The children are shown the kinds of things each would say (the OK lady would say acceptable sentences such as "A boy eats an apple"; the silly lady would say unacceptable sentences such as "An apple eats a boy"). Test sentences are then read to the child, who is asked to point to the lady who would say each one to indicate a judgment about the acceptability of each sentence. Procedure 4.2 in this chapter is based on this method.

A second variation of the judgment task extends beyond asking the child to identify OK or silly sentences. This extension requires the child to convert the unacceptable sentences to acceptable ones. As Table 1.4 showed, the correction tasks add yet another level of difficulty to this comprehension method. Children can identify silly sentences appropriately before they can correct them accurately.

Judgment tasks can be used to assess children's knowledge of either semantic or syntactic acceptability. Semantic acceptability can be assessed at the level of individual semantic features by violating only one selection–restriction rule in each sentence ("The pretty girl smiled" versus "The furry girl smiled"; "The spider crawled across the room" versus "The spider skated across the room"), or at a more global level, such as that used in the *Verbal Absurdities* subtest of the *Detroit Tests of Learning Aptitude–III* (Hammill, 1992) (e.g., "My mom always makes us eat breakfast before we wake up"). Syntactic abilities can also be assessed with a judgment task. De Villiers and de Villiers (1973) asked children to judge the acceptability of sentences such as "tooth your brush" and "cake the eat." As Table 1.4 showed, semantic anomalies are identified by children earlier than these syntactic ones.

Finally, a semantic acceptability judgment task can be used to infer syntactic comprehension. For example, Paul (1985) used a procedure that required children to judge semantic acceptability in order to test their syntactic comprehension of active ("A boy rides a bike"), passive ("A bike is ridden by a boy"), and cleft-agent ("It's a boy who rides a bike") sentences. Examples of the three sentence types were presented in probable ("A boy rides a bike") and reversed ("A bike rides a boy") forms. Children were taught to identify silly and OK sentences by pointing to the silly or OK lady pictures. In order to decide which sentences were silly or OK, it was necessary for the children to use the syntactic form of the sentence to label agents and objects of action appropriately. This procedure allows the clinician to sample a variety of sentence forms using a relatively large number of examples for each one, while saving the time and expense of drawing a picture for each stimulus.

EXPECTATIONS FOR THE L4L STAGE

The procedures in this chapter include suggestions of some syntactic forms, semantic concepts, and discourse functions that are expected to emerge in the L4L developmental stage, are rarely sampled on standardized tests, and can add significantly to our understanding of the receptive abilities of children in the elementary school grades. In addition, Table 4.1 gives an extended list of semantic domains that can be considered for additional informal testing at this level. The procedures given here are meant to serve as examples of flexible tools for constructing assessment for specific children and to test narrowly defined sets of items that are likely to be important for success in school. In addition, these methods have been particularly helpful in probing the comprehension of new content introduced in intervention where the testing method should be different from the teaching method.

Table 4.1. Possible semantic domains for testing and teaching

Domain	Examples
Major semantic categories	
Quantity	More, less, equal, half, while, great, grand, vast, abundance, small, little, trace, smidgen, increase, decrease, add, subtract
Number	Some, few, couple, (count 1–20), double, triple, century, hundred, thousand (Piagetian math books)
Order	First, second, and so forth; next
Time	Day, week, month, winter, summer, spring, fall, second, minute, hour, yesterday, tomorrow, year, now, later, present, past, future, young, old, new, early, late, morning, noon, nighttime, tonight, wait, when, while, again, after, before, anytime, ever, finally, finish, frequently, last, seldom, someday, until, usually
Change	Transform, fix, permanent, stable, substitute, reverse, return, same, difference, escape
Cause	Power, strength, weak, activate, frail, energy, force, drive, run, act on, operate
Form	Size, shape, equal, square, circle, rectangle, triangle, round, straight, cube, angle, sharp, smooth, rough, blunt
Location (space)	In, on, under, beside, behind, front, between, through, below, before, after, around, inside, over, vertical, rear, prone, level, left, right, near, horizontal, flush, edge, foreground, background, among, adjacent, adjoining, slope
Motion action verbs	
Location/change	Come, go, leave, walk, skip, trot, jump, run, hop, crawl, climb, drive
Action on object	Heat, mix, stir, shake, drop, kick, hit, push, chase, kiss, hug, spill, pour, touch, chop, cut, grab
Object transfer	Bring, take, give, get, buy, sell, trade, put, carry
Object consumption	Eat, drink, swallow, gulp, chew, bite
Object creation	Make, build, cook, draw, write, sew
Object destruction	Break, burn, kill, tear down, smash
Activity	Dance, fight, fish, count, dress, work, swim
Other actions	Sneeze, cough, laugh, cry, giggle, smile, whistle, breathe, wink, grin, look, stare
Performatives	Marry, divorce, adopt, join
Communication	Ask, tell, promise, say, report, call, question, speak, talk, discuss
Process verbs	
Changes of state	Happen, change, become, grow, dry, fall, die, appear, disappear
State verbs	
Perceiving	See, hear, smell, notice, read, feel, taste
Knowing (mental)	Remember, forget, fuss, think, know, learn, imagine, pretend, wonder, suspect, believe, bet, certain, decide, figure, except, guess, hope, maybe, might, perhaps, probably, remind, seems, suppose, surprise, thought, understand, wish
Feeling	Love, like, hate, need, want, feel, wish
Locative state	Stay, remain, wait, stand, sit, lean
Rest state	Rest, sleep, relax, lounge

The procedures given here are designed for assessing discourse comprehension and comprehension of classroom language during this stage. Discourse comprehension skills expected of the school-age child include the ability to judge the appropriateness of certain speech styles in context, the ability to recognize given (from new) information in complex sentence forms, and a host of metalinguistic abilities that both contribute to, and are formed by, learning to read. Knowledge of vocabulary and sentence types used in teachers' language can also be assessed (Paul, 1995).

PREPARATION
FOR ASSESSMENT

In order to proceed with using the methods detailed in this chapter, you will need to do the following:

1. Review developmental production data (e.g., Haynes & Shulman, 1994; Miller, 1981; Owens, 1992) and the comprehension data presented in Chapter 2 of this book. These data provide content sequences for vocabulary and syntax for a variety of linguistic forms.
2. Practice giving each procedure before you use it clinically.
3. Set up your testing session so that more than one procedure can be used to test the same content where possible. This will allow you options when the child, for some unforeseen reason, is unable to perform your first choice task.
4. Observe a child in the classroom, note features of the teacher's language that may be problematic, and test the child's understanding of these forms in criterion-referenced procedures. These features of curriculum-based assessment (Nelson, 1993) can be helpful in testing understanding of teachers' language.

◇ # Examining Individual Syntactic Structures in Object Manipulation Tasks

---

DEVELOPMENTAL LEVEL	4–8 years

LINGUISTIC LEVEL   Syntactic/morphological

LINGUISTIC STIMULI   Sentences from Bellugi-Klima (1968) (see score sheet on pp. 156–158)

RESPONSE TYPE   Object manipulation

MATERIALS

1. Negative versus Affirmative Statements
   Set A: • Two dolls, one with movable arms and one with arms that cannot move
   Set B: • Two dolls, one seated and one standing
   Set C: • Two dolls, one with a hat and one without a hat
2. Negative versus Affirmative Questions
   Set A: • A pile of approximately six objects, some edible and some inedible (e.g., cookies, vegetables, cars, blocks, dolls)
   Set B: • Girl doll
         • Doll clothing
         • Approximately six nonclothing objects
3. Singular versus Plural with Noun and Verb Inflection
   Set A: • Two girl dolls
   Set B: • Two boy dolls
4. Modification (adjectives)
   Set A: • Two balls, one large and one small
         • Two boy dolls, one large and one small
   Set B: • Two buttons, one round and one square
         • Two blocks, one round and one square
5. Sentence versus Adverbial Negation
         • Several blocks, some large and some small
6. Negative Affixes
   Set A: • Several blocks
   Set B: • Several blocks
7. Reflexivation
         • Two boy dolls
         • A washcloth
8. Reflexivation versus Reciprocal
         • Two boy dolls
         • Two washcloths

9. Comparatives

Set A: *more* versus *less*
- One boy doll
- One girl doll
- Several marbles
- Clay

Set B: *-er* endings
- Sticks of various lengths and thicknesses

10. Reversible Passives
- Toy cat
- Toy dog
- Boy doll
- Girl doll

11. Nonreversible Passives
- One girl doll
- Toy cup
- One apple
- One boy doll

12. Conjunctions

Set A: *and* versus *or*
- Blocks of various shapes (circle and square must be included)

Set B: *either* versus *neither*
- Blocks of various shapes (circle and square must be included)

13. Self-Embedded Sentences

Set A: • Toy cat
- Toy dog

Set B: • Girl doll
- Boy doll
- Toy telephone

Set C: • Toy cat
- Toy dog

Set D: • Toy cat
- Toy dog

PROCEDURE

1. Review the stimulus sentences on the score sheet on pages 156–158, and select the sets appropriate for the child to be tested. You may not want to test all 13 categories of sentences or all of the sets within the categories; instead, you may want to test only those categories the child needs to understand to succeed in the classroom. These could be identified by means of a curriculum-based assessment (Nelson, 1992). To conduct such an assessment, observe the child in the classroom, noting forms on the score sheet on pages 156–158 that are used by the teacher and observing whether the child appears to have difficulty responding to specific sentence types.

2. Gather the materials necessary for each set to be used in the test. Note that substitutions may be made according to availability of materials and the child's known vocabulary. For example, to test the sixth category, negative affixes, you may substitute bottles and corks or dresses with snaps for blocks. If you make such substitutions, be

sure to modify the stimulus sentences accordingly, as in:

"Show me: 'The bottles are corked.'"
"Show me: 'The bottles are uncorked.'"

or

"Show me: 'The dresses are snapped.'"
"Show me: 'The dresses are unsnapped.'"

3. If necessary, depending on the specific test set, arrange the materials. For example, Category 1, Set B requires one doll to be in a seated position and the other to be in a standing position. Where special material arrangements are necessary, they are noted on the score sheet on pages 156–158.

    Before each stimulus item in a set, return the materials to their original positions.

4. For each set, present the child with the materials.
5. Read the stimulus sentences one at a time.
6. Record the child's responses on a score sheet like the one on pages 156–158.

PASSING RESPONSE

The child responds correctly to all items within a set. If the child makes errors on any item within a set, retest the item on which the error was made twice. If the child responds correctly on *both* retests, score the item as correct. Any set in which the child makes an error on one or more items that is not responded to correctly on both retests should be considered as a target for intervention.

DIAGNOSTIC NOTE

Bellugi-Klima's (1968) forms are acquired by typically developing children toward the end of the preschool period and in the early school years. They may be difficult for school-age children with language learning disabilities.

PROCEDURE
4.2   ◇   Protocol for Judgment Task
for Assessing Comprehension
of Passive Sentences

DEVELOPMENTAL LEVEL   6–9 years

LINGUISTIC LEVEL   Syntactic

LINGUISTIC STIMULI   Passive sentences

RESPONSE TYPE   Contrived—judgment

MATERIALS   • "OK lady" and "Silly lady" pictures (see p. 147)

PROCEDURE

1. Tell the child, "I have two ladies here [show both pictures]. This lady [point to "OK lady" picture] is a regular, OK lady. She says OK things like:

> 'A boy eats an apple.'
> 'A man drives a truck.'
> 'A girl rides a bike.'"

2. Tell the child, "But this other lady [point to "silly lady" picture] is a silly lady. She says silly things like:

> 'An apple eats a boy.'
> 'A truck drives the man.'
> 'A bike rides a girl.'
> 'An orange squeezes a girl.'"

3. Give the child the following instructions: "I'll say some things. You point to the lady you think would say each one."

4. Read each of the following practice items to the child. Give the child time to point to one of the pictures. (The correct answers are given in parentheses following each stimulus item.) If the child provides correct responses to all six practice items, move on to the stimulus sentences. If the child responds incorrectly to the practice items, review the instructions, pointing out what makes one or two examples "silly " or "OK." Then administer the remaining practice items. If the child still has difficulty, you should consider this procedure, with its task–response method, too difficult and use alternate methods such as picture-pointing and object manipulation tasks.

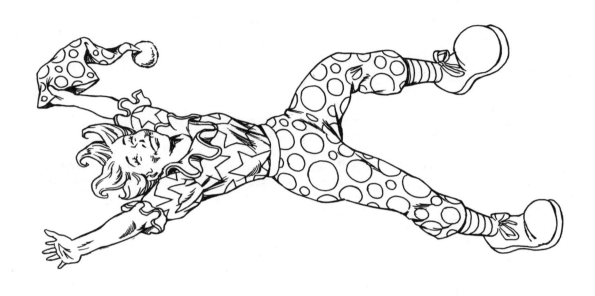

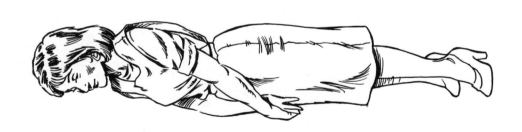

"A woman eats an orange." (OK)
"A man jumps over a fence." (OK)
"A car bites a train." (Silly)
"A dog chases a cat." (OK)
"A banana opens a door." (Silly)
"A table kicks a boy." (Silly)

5. Proceed to the stimulus items on the score sheet on page 159.
6. Record the child's responses on a score sheet like the one on page 159.

PASSING RESPONSE

In a study of typically developing school children with mixed socioeconomic status, Paul (1985) found that all of the 8- to 12-year-old children tested on this task performed at better than 90% correct. Six- and 7-year-old children showed a more inconsistent pattern of responding to passive sentences. If a child with a developmental level above 8 years scores less than 90% on this task, passive sentences can be considered a target for intervention.

| PROCEDURE | ◇ | Recognizing |
| 4.3 | | Appropriate Speech Styles |

DEVELOPMENTAL LEVEL   5–12 years

LINGUISTIC LEVEL   Discourse

LINGUISTIC STIMULI   Role-play conversations

RESPONSE TYPE   Contrived—judgment

MATERIALS   • Assorted puppets

PROCEDURE

1. Tell the child that the puppets will play various characters in a movie and that the child is the director and must tell the puppets if they are playing their characters correctly.

2. For each movie scenario, assign a role to each puppet, present the short bits of dialogue (like those given below in the examples) between the two puppets, and ask the child, "Did they do it OK? Which one was wrong? How should the puppet talk?"

Example movie 1:   Roles: Teacher (Miss Jones), student (Johnny)
Teacher: Good morning, Johnny. Did you do your homework last night?
Johnny: Yes, Miss Jones, but my dog ate it when I left it on the kitchen table.

Example movie 2:   Roles: Doctor, patient.
Patient: Doc, my throat's really sore today.
Doctor: Your throat's sore? Hey fella, mine is killing me.

Example movie 3:   Roles: Mother, daughter
Mother: Jane, you really should clean up your room.
Jane: Well, honey, I'll try to get to it for you by beddy-bye time.

Example movie 4:   Roles: Two friends (Jack and Jim)
Jack: Let's have a race around the block!
Jim: Well, you know, son, it really isn't wise to use excessive speed on the sidewalk.

3. Record the child's responses on a score sheet like the one on page 160.

PASSING RESPONSE

The child should make all judgments correctly to "pass" this procedure. Children younger than 9 years may not be able to provide corrected responses and should be considered to pass without them. Children older than 9 years should be able to judge all scenarios correctly and provide an appropriate condition.

PROCEDURE
4.4 ◇ **Criterion-Referenced Assessment of Center-Embedded Relative Clauses**

DEVELOPMENTAL LEVEL	8–12 years
LINGUISTIC LEVEL	Syntactic
LINGUISTIC STIMULI	Sentences (like those given on the score sheet on p. 161) with center-embedded relative clauses, which are often difficult for children with language disorders
RESPONSE TYPE	Contrived—yes/no judgments
MATERIALS	None
PROCEDURE	1. Present stimulus sentences like those provided on the score sheet on page 161 and ask the child to answer each question. 2. Record the child's responses on a score sheet like the one on page 161.
PASSING RESPONSE	The child interprets a majority of the sentences correctly.

◇ # Comprehension of Spatial, Temporal, and Connective Terms in Classroom Vocabulary

---

DEVELOPMENTAL LEVEL   6–12 years

LINGUISTIC LEVEL   Lexical

LINGUISTIC STIMULI   Sentences (like those below) containing words used in classroom language that seem, from a previously done curriculum-based assessment (Nelson, 1993), to give the child trouble

RESPONSE TYPE   Natural—behavioral compliance

MATERIALS

Set 1:   Spatial Terms
- Piece of paper with a sticker in the middle
- Pencil

Set 2:   Temporal Terms
- Whistle, bell, or other noise maker

Set 3:   Connective Terms
- Whistle, bell, or other noise maker

PROCEDURE

1. Review the stimulus sentences for each set below and select the sets appropriate for the child to be tested.
2. Gather the materials necessary for each set to be used in the test.
3. For each set, give the child the materials gathered.
4. Give the child the instructions in each example set, one at a time, or give instructions like those given in the example sets. Give three instructions for each italicized term, interspersing the items so the three similar instructions are *not* given consecutively. Note the child's responses to each on a score sheet like the one on page 162. (Note also that the three scores for each item are listed together on the score sheet for convenience. In administering the instructions, however, be sure to mix up the instructions to avoid giving the same type of item consecutively.)

Example set 1:   Spatial Terms
   a. Make dots *above* the sticker.
   b. Make dots *below* the sticker.

        c. Make dots *around* the sticker.
        d. Make dots to the *right* of the sticker.
        e. Make dots *beside* the sticker.
        f. Make dots *on the left-hand side* of the sticker.

Example set 2:   Temporal Terms
        a. Make a noise *after* I say "Go." (Pause before saying "Go.")
        b. Make a noise *before* I say "Go." (Pause before saying "Go.")
        c. Make a noise *while* I say "Go." (Say "Go.")
        d. Make a noise *as* I say "Go." (Say "Go.")
        e. Make a noise *when* I say "Go." (Say "Go.")

Example set 3:   Connective Terms
        a. Make a noise *if* I say "Go." (Say "Go.")
        b. Make a noise *although* I say "Go." (Say "Go.")
        c. Make a noise *unless* I say "Go." (Say "Go.")
        d. Make a noise *until* I say "Go." (Pause before saying "Go.")

PASSING RESPONSE   The child performs correctly on three trials for each vocabulary item.

◇ # Criterion-Referenced Assessment of Classroom Direction Vocabulary

---

DEVELOPMENTAL LEVEL
6–12 years

LINGUISTIC LEVEL
Lexical/syntactic

LINGUISTIC STIMULI
Sentences (like those below) containing language from teachers' instructions that seem, from a previously done curriculum-based assessment (Nelson, 1993), to give the student trouble

RESPONSE TYPE
Natural—behavioral compliance

MATERIALS
- Piece of paper
- Pencil

PROCEDURE
1. Review the instructions below and select those appropriate for the child to be tested. It may be necessary to observe the child in the classroom and to note teacher directives with which the child seems to have trouble (i.e., perform a curriculum-based assessment). The examples given below should be supplemented with those the clinician identifies through such a curriculum-based assessment (Nelson, 1992).

2. Tell the child:

   Let's pretend you're a soldier. You're a good soldier. You always do what the sergeant says. Here's some paperwork the sergeant wants you to take care of. I'll be the sergeant and give some orders. You follow the sergeant's orders and write what the sergeant says to write on this paper. Listen carefully, now! Here we go!

3. Give the child instructions such as the following, one at a time. After each give the child time to complete the task.
   a. OK, Private, draw a star in an *upper right-hand corner* of the paper.
   b. Now, Private, draw a tank on the *right-hand side* of the paper.
   c. Write today's *date*, Private.
   d. *Number* your paper from 1 to 10.
   e. All right, Private, draw a line down the *left side* of the paper.
   f. Now put a square in the *upper left-hand corner*.

4. Record the child's responses on a score sheet like the one on page 163.

PASSING RESPONSE

The child follows directions correctly. Any direction on which the child makes an error can be given again. If the child responds incorrectly the second time, consider the item as an intervention target. If the child responds to the second trial correctly, give the item again after an interval. If the child responds correctly on this trial, consider the item passed. If not, consider this a target for intervention.

◇ SCORE SHEET
Grammatical Forms for
Testing by Object Manipulation

Instructions: For each set administered to the child, indicate the child's response in the right column opposite the stimulus item. If you substitute materials, and therefore stimulus sentences, mark changes in the left column to reflect these substitutions.

Child's name: _____

Child's chronological age (years.months): _____

Date: _____

Forms	Child's response
1. Negative versus Affirmative Statements with Auxiliaries	
Set A:	
"Show me: 'The doll can't put his arms down.'"	
"Show me: 'The doll can put his arms down.'"	
Set B:	
Note: Arrange dolls so one is sitting and one is not.	
"Show me: 'The doll is sitting.'"	
"Show me: 'The doll is not sitting.'"	
Set C:	
Note: Arrange dolls so one is wearing a hat and one is not.	
"Show me: 'The doll doesn't have a hat.'"	
"Show me: 'The doll has a hat.'"	
2. Negative versus Affirmative Questions	
Set A:	
"What can't you eat?"	
"What can you eat?"	
Set B:	
"What does she wear?"	
"What doesn't she wear?"	

The Clinical Assessment of Language Comprehension
by Jon F. Miller and Rhea Paul   © 1995 Paul H. Brookes Publishing Co., Baltimore

Forms	Child's response
3. Singular versus Plural with Noun and Verb Inflection	

Set A:

Note: Begin with both dolls lying down. Demonstrate walking for the child.

"Show me: 'The girl walks.'"

"Show me: 'The girls walk.'"

Set B:

"Show me: 'The boy jumps.'"

"Show me: 'The boys jump.'"

4. Modification

Set A:

"Give the little boy a big ball."

"Give the big boy a little ball."

Set B:

"Put the round button on the square block."

"Put the square button on the round block."

5. Sentence versus Adverbial Negation

Note: Place some large blocks on top of small blocks, some small blocks on top of large blocks, and some blocks separate from the others (perhaps five of each type of arrangement).

"Show me: 'No little blocks are on big blocks.'"

"Show me: 'No, the little blocks are on the big blocks.'"

6. Negative Affixes

Set A:

Note: Arrange the blocks so some are piled on top of one another and some are lying separate from the others.

"Show me: 'The blocks are piled.'"

"Show me: 'The blocks are unpiled.'"

Set B:

"Show me: 'The blocks are not unpiled.'"

7. Reflexivation

Note: Demonstrate washing for the child. Introduce the dolls as John and Bill.

"Show me: 'John washed him.'"

"Show me: 'John washed himself.'"

The Clinical Assessment of Language Comprehension
by Jon F. Miller and Rhea Paul   © 1995 Paul H. Brookes Publishing Co., Baltimore

Forms	Child's response
8. Reflexivation versus Reciprocal *Note:* Demonstrate washing for the child. "Show me: 'They washed themselves.'" "Show me: 'They washed each other.'"	
9. Comparatives Set A: *more* versus *less* "Show me: 'The boy has more marbles than the girl.'" "Show me: 'The boy has less clay than the girl.'" Set B: *-er* endings *Note:* Hold up one stick for each item in the set. "Give me a stick that is shorter and thicker than this one." "Give me a stick that is longer and thicker than this one."	
10. Reversible Passives "The cat is chased by the dog." "The boy is washed by the girl." "The girl is pushed by the boy."	
11. Nonreversible Passives "The milk is drunk by the girl." "The apple is eaten by the boy."	
12. Conjunctions Set A: *and* versus *or* "Give me a circle or a square." "Give me a circle and a square." Set B: *either* versus *neither* "Give me a piece that is neither a circle nor a square." "Give me a piece that is either a circle or a square."	
13. Self-Embedded Sentences Set A: "The cat that the dog chased jumped." Set B: "The girl that the boy phoned stood up." Set C: "The cat that the dog chased jumped." "The cat that chased the dog jumped." Set D: "Before he jumped he fell down." "He jumped before he fell down."	
Copyright, Ursula Bellugi, The Salk Institute, La Jolla, CA.	

<table>
<tr><td>FOR USE WITH
PROCEDURE:
4.2</td></tr>
</table>

SCORE SHEET
◇ Assessing Comprehension
of Passive Sentences
with Judgment Tasks

Instructions: For each stimulus sentence, indicate the child's response in the far-right column.

Child's name: _____

Child's chronological age (years.months): _____

Date: _____

Stimulus sentences	Correct response	Child's response
"A train is started by a man."	OK	
"A toy paints a boy."	S	
"A table moves a man."	S	
"A wagon wrecks a man."	S	
"A woman is peeled by an orange."	S	
"A toy picks a woman."	S	
"A girl is washed by a floor."	S	
"A tree plants a boy."	S	
"An orange is peeled by a woman."	OK	
"A man is started by a train."	S	
"A floor is washed by a girl."	OK	
"A boy carries an ice cream."	OK	
"A wagon is fixed by a boy."	OK	
"A girl is pulled by a wagon."	S	
"A boy is fixed by a wagon."	S	
"A boy moves a table."	OK	
"A man is lifted by a table."	S	
"A wheel is turned by a man."	OK	
"A wagon is pulled by a girl."	OK	
"A boy plants a tree."	OK	
"A house cleans a girl."	S	
"An ice cream carries a boy."	S	
"A woman picks a toy."	OK	
"A table is lifted by a man."	OK	
"A man is turned by a wheel."	S	
"A girl cleans a house."	OK	
"A man paints a toy."	OK	
"A man wrecks a wagon."	OK	

Scoring key: S = Silly lady
OK = OK lady

The Clinical Assessment of Language Comprehension
by Jon F. Miller and Rhea Paul   © 1995 Paul H. Brookes Publishing Co., Baltimore

<table>
<tr><td>FOR USE WITH PROCEDURE: 4.3</td><td>◇ </td><td># SCORE SHEET
Appropriate
Speech Styles</td></tr>
</table>

Instructions: For each movie scenario, record the child's judgment of the dialogue as OK or NOT OK in the third column. If the child indicates that the dialogue is NOT OK, write in the far-right column what he or she says to correct the dialogue.

Child's name: _____

Child's chronological age (years.months): _____

Date: _____

Movie scenario	Correct judgment	Child's judgment	Child's correction of NOT OK dialogue
1	OK		
2	NOT OK		
3	NOT OK		
4	NOT OK		

The Clinical Assessment of Language Comprehension
by Jon F. Miller and Rhea Paul   © 1995 Paul H. Brookes Publishing Co., Baltimore

◇ SCORE SHEET
Criterion-Referenced
Assessment of
Center-Embedded Relative Clauses

Instructions: For each stimulus sentence and subsequent question, record the child's response (yes or no) in the far-right column.

Child's name: _____

Child's chronological age (years.months): _____

Date: _____

Stimulus sentence	Question	Correct answer	Child's answer
The boy who chased the cow was wearing a hat.	Was the cow wearing a hat?	No	
The girl who rode the pony was named Sally.	Was the pony named Sally?	No	
The crook who ran from the police officer was carrying a bag.	Was the crook carrying a bag?	Yes	
The woman who lost her dog was wearing a sweater.	Was the dog wearing a sweater?	No	
The cat that chased the dog was brown.	Was the dog brown?	No	
The cow that bit the goat was called Sadie.	Was the cow called Sadie?	Yes	

The Clinical Assessment of Language Comprehension
by Jon F. Miller and Rhea Paul   © 1995 Paul H. Brookes Publishing Co., Baltimore

<table>
<tr><td rowspan="2" style="border:1px solid">FOR USE WITH PROCEDURE: 4.5</td></tr>
</table>

◇ # SCORE SHEET
Comprehension of Spatial, Temporal, and Connective Terms

Instructions: For each trial, indicate the child's response to the stimulus items. For items you create, fill in the second column with the stimulus item, highlighting in some way (e.g., underlining) the specific spatial, temporal, or connective term you are specifically testing.

Child's name: _____

Child's chronological age (years.months): _____

Date: _____

Set of terms	Stimulus item	Child's response/trial		
		1	2	3
1. Spatial	a. Make dots *above* the sticker.			
	b. Make dots *below* the sticker.			
	c. Make dots *around* the sticker.			
	d. Make dots to the *right* of the sticker.			
	e. Make dots *beside* the sticker.			
	f. Make dots *on the left-hand side* of the sticker.			
	g.			
	h.			
	i.			
2. Temporal	a. Make a noise *after* I say "Go."			
	b. Make a noise *before* I say "Go."			
	c. Make a noise *while* I say "Go."			
	d. Make a noise *as* I say "Go."			
	e. Make a noise *when* I say "Go."			
	f.			
	g.			
	h.			
3. Connective	a. Make a noise *if* I say "Go."			
	b. Make a noise *although* I say "Go."			
	c. Make a noise *unless* I say "Go."			
	d. Make a noise *until* I say "Go."			
	e.			
	f.			
	g.			

Scoring key: + = Child follows directions correctly
 − = Child follows directions incorrectly
 NR = Child gives no response

The Clinical Assessment of Language Comprehension
by Jon F. Miller and Rhea Paul © 1995 Paul H. Brookes Publishing Co., Baltimore

162

<table>
<tr><td>FOR USE WITH
PROCEDURE:
4.6</td></tr>
</table>

FOR USE WITH PROCEDURE: 4.6	**SCORE SHEET** **Criterion-Referenced Assessment** **of Classroom Direction Vocabulary**

Instructions: For each stimulus item, indicate the child's response in the right column. For items you create, fill in the left column with the stimulus item for which you are testing (e.g., the specific directive word or phrase).

Child's name: _____

Child's chronological age (years.months): _____

Date: _____

Classroom vocabulary item	Child's response
a. Upper right-hand corner	
b. Right-hand side	
c. Date	
d. Number	
e. Left side	
f. Upper left-hand corner	
g.	
h.	
i.	
j.	
k.	
l.	

Scoring key:　　+ = Child answers correctly
　　　　　　　　　− = Child answers incorrectly
　　　　　　　　　NR = Child gives no response

The Clinical Assessment of Language Comprehension
by Jon F. Miller and Rhea Paul　© 1995 Paul H. Brookes Publishing Co., Baltimore

5 ◇ Case Studies in Comprehension Assessment

To illustrate how the model of comprehension assessment presented in this book can be implemented for children in each of the three developmental stages, the following case studies are provided. This chapter also addresses comprehension assessment for children with severe speech impairments.

THE EMERGING LANGUAGE STAGE

Jaime

When Jaime was 18 months old, his mother reported that he didn't say any words. Is this a problem? It may be or it may not be. Paul's (1993) data suggest that 18 months of age may be too young to decide whether a child with a circumscribed expressive delay has a problem. However, if both expression *and* comprehension are delayed, there may be more cause for concern. To determine whether Jaime has a language impairment that merits attention, we need to have his hearing tested carefully and then assess his receptive skills. Here is an outline of the assessment plan for Jaime and its results.

Assessment Plan: Step 1

Assess communicative ability by observing Jaime playing with a familiar person. Count the number of times he initiates communication, either verbally or nonverbally. (See Paul [1995] and Wetherby and Prizant [1990] for detailed communication assessment procedures.)

Does Jaime communicate and, if so, how? To answer this question, we must observe Jaime for gestures, vocalizations, gestures *and* vocalizations, and words. Jaime's range of communicative functions (e.g., requests, comments) should also be examined. It is useful to record frequencies of productions. During the emerging language stage of development, this can often be done without video recording equipment because productions are infrequent. (Wetherby, Cain, Yonclas, and Walker [1988] reported an average of two intentions per minute at 18 months and five per minute at 24 months in typically developing children.)

Results

Initial observation of Jaime confirmed his mother's observations. No intelligible words were observed, and only vowels were produced. We did observe, though, that Jaime was active and communicated a range of intentions, with normal frequency for his age.

Assessment Plan: Step 2

To assess Jaime's comprehension, the following steps should be taken:

1. Look at literal comprehension of single words using Procedures 2.3 and 2.5. If Jaime does not respond appropriately to any single

words, determine which, if any, response strategies he uses by asking for an item while pointing and looking at it. If he responds using a "look at what the adult looks at" strategy, credit him with the use of this strategy. If Jaime does not use this strategy, terminate receptive testing.

2.   If Jaime has literal comprehension for some single words, assess comprehension of word combinations using Procedure 2.6. If Jaime does not respond appropriately, examine responses for use of the "do what you usually do" (i.e., conventional use of objects) strategy. If he does not comprehend unusual two-word combinations and does not use this strategy, terminate comprehension assessment.

3.   If Jaime comprehends unusual two-word instructions or uses a "do what you usually do" strategy, test comprehension of three-word instructions using Procedure 3.3. If Jaime succeeds at this task, terminate comprehension assessment because comprehension is clearly ahead of production. If Jaime fails the two-word task, examine responses for evidence of the "child-as-agent" strategy. Use of this strategy indicates discourse-level comprehension because Jaime would, in using it, be responding to the discourse-level intent of the utterance (i.e., a request for action) even though he was not able to process all of the literal meaning of the utterance.

Results

Jaime's hearing was within normal limits. He demonstrated comprehension of object and person names and some verbs. He did not comprehend words for absent objects, but did understand two-word utterances, including possessor-possession. This is a common outcome where comprehension appears to be appropriate but production skills are marginal. Given the wide variability in rates of progress in production, it is not possible to determine whether production is delayed at this age. Jaime's relatively good comprehension is a reassuring sign. Before making a decision about intervention, we should review all the reasons this child's production may be lagging. Speech motor limitations should be assessed, for example. We might then provide his parents with some information about language stimulation techniques and suggest they try using scaffolded book reading and indirect language stimulation (see Paul [1995] for details) at home. We would want to see Jaime again when he is 24 months old. If production has not improved by then, the need for intervention should be reviewed with parents.

Ashley

Ashley is a 34-month-old girl with Down syndrome. Her mother reports that Ashley produces no intelligible words at this point.

We know that cognitive impairments are associated with Down syndrome and research has documented that comprehension skills are generally better than production (Miller, 1987b, 1988, 1992). Otitis media is frequent and persistent in this population, so ongoing hearing evaluation is especially important. To begin, we would review Ashley's production status, as we did with Jaime. We would also need information about her developmental level. If cognitive testing is not available, we can use play assessment to estimate cognitive level (see Paul [1995] for details of play assessment procedures). As a last resort, we can use the rule of thumb for mental age being one half chronological age (Miller, Leavitt, & Leddy, in press). Previous testing had revealed Ashley's developmental age to be about 24 months. Here is an assessment plan for Ashley and its results.

Assessment Plan: Step 1

Assess communicative ability as we did in the first step of Jaime's plan. Because parents of children with Down syndrome often engage in routines to demonstrate their child's best performances, suggest at the outset, "We would like to see Ashley play on her own for a few minutes. Try to respond to her without leading the activity."

Results

Ashley was only producing two vowels. She exhibited intentional communication through gesture only. Only request intentions were observed, and these were low in frequency.

Assessment Plan: Step 2

Begin comprehension assessment with Procedure 2.2 because joint reference is critical for word learning. Procedure 2.3, comprehension of object and person names, will be the major focus. If Ashley is successful, move to Procedure 2.4, comprehension of action words. If verbs are understood, then Procedures 2.5 and 2.6 can be administered because for children with Down syndrome production may be very delayed relative to comprehension status. An estimate of language level based only on production may be an underestimate.

Results

Ashley demonstrated frequent joint reference to objects with her mother, and comprehension of a wide range of object and person names. Only the verbs "hug" and "kiss" were understood.

No success was observed on the initial items from Procedures 2.5 and 2.6. No strategies were observed; Ashley simply did not respond to words for absent objects or to two-word combinations. This suggests that her discourse-level comprehension is as impaired as her literal comprehension skills. In a case such as this, where communication, literal and discourse comprehension, and production are delayed relative to developmental level, we need to build a strong base in communicative intention and receptive skills before focusing on the formal aspects of production. We would concentrate first on increasing communicative attempts through communication temptations (Wetherby & Prizant, 1989) and building receptive skill through facilitative play and indirect language stimulation (Fey, 1986). If frustration with production is evident, we might evaluate the use of sign instruction with Ashley's parents and teachers. We would need to be aware of the limitations of sign instruction (Miller, 1992), though, and carefully review all other potential limitations on production performance (see Swift and Rosin [1990] for intervention advice). Children with Down syndrome frequently have low intelligibility for the first 3–4 years of life. We may want to concentrate on other areas of language development during this early period and focus on intelligibility when Ashley is 5 years old.

THE DEVELOPING LANGUAGE STAGE

The developing language stage is probably the most active in terms of the amount of language learned, with vocabularies approaching 5,000 words, the majority of syntax being acquired, and discourse-level skills and semantic diversity expanding dramatically. Still, children in this age range are inconsistent in their ability to stay focused and respond consistently in testing situations. The procedures in Chapter 3 provide basic testing methods for the first half of this stage, as well as procedures that can supplement standardized testing for children at the later segment of this period. Assessing children at this level of development requires consideration across language domains, including discourse, syntax, and semantics.

Peter

Peter is a 5-year-old boy with hearing and cognitive skills within the normal range and an MLU of 2.3. He produces a restricted number of different words on a 100-utterance language sample (more than –2 SDs from the mean on both measures). Because both of these measures correlate highly with age, these data suggest a significant delay in acquiring production skills. In addition, Peter produces far less language per unit time than his peers, requiring more than 5 minutes longer to produce his language sample. We can expect that Peter's comprehension performance could range from being consistent with his production skills to equivalent or slightly better than his chronological age. We would proceed to evaluate Peter's comprehension as follows.

Assessment Plan

Begin with Procedures 3.1, understanding illocutionary intent in requests, and 3.2, inferring and continuing topics. Data from Procedure 3.2 can be taken from the language sample. Then move to Procedure 3.3 to evaluate two- and three-word S-V and S-V-O utterances. Administer Procedure 3.4. Use a free-play context for Procedure 3.8 because a structured format may seem too contrived to test Peter's question comprehension. If the role-playing task appears too cognitively demanding for Peter, Procedure 3.7 can be used. It will also give us some notion as to whether Peter can respond to a picture format. Attempt Procedures 3.10, 3.11, and 3.13. Review the language sample for evidence of success on Procedure 3.12 because several requests for clarification will be made.

Results

Peter had no difficulty with understanding the illocutionary intent of requests (Procedure 3.1) or following topics (Procedure 3.2) in natural conversation. All of his utterances were judged to follow the topic appropriately, placing him at or above the 3-year level of performance. He exhibited little difficulty with two- and three-word instructions (Procedure 3.3) and also passed 95% of the items on the word order comprehension task (Procedure 3.7), indicating syntactic comprehension at least at the 3- to 4-year-old level. Because he could perform with the picture format, other picture tests (e.g., *Peabody Picture Vocabulary Test–Revised [PPVT–R]*) could be used with him. Peter also performed the locative search task (Procedure 3.4) flawlessly, suggesting 4-year level performance. He was able to respond to questions (Procedure 3.8) appropriately through "how?" and "how much?", which are at a 4.0+

level of performance. He had no difficulty in responding to requests for clarification.

In summary, Peter is performing at least at the 4-year level of comprehension at all levels tested in syntax, semantics, and discourse. This suggests that language comprehension is synchronous across areas. Peter's comprehension skills are far better than his production skills. In light of these findings, we would need to evaluate his nonverbal cognitive status. It would also be useful to examine his vocabulary abilities using the *PPVT–R* (Dunn & Dunn, 1981) or a vocabulary definition task like that on the *Test of Language Development–2 Primary (TOLD–R)* (Newcomer & Hammill, 1988) because vocabulary problems cannot be ruled out by the data gathered so far. A small vocabulary was used deliberately in order to avoid underestimating general receptive skills on the basis of small vocabulary. There are remaining questions, including whether other factors, such as environmental events or speech motor limitations, might be responsible for Peter's limited production skills. After a thorough speech motor assessment, we might want to try some parent training and reevaluate results in 3 months. If improvement is not seen, more direct intervention can be considered.

THE LANGUAGE FOR LEARNING STAGE

Assessment at the L4L level generally includes some standardized testing, because children can perform both picture-pointing and object manipulation formats. In addition, judgment tasks can be added to the procedure repertoire. Judgment tasks provide considerable flexibility in developing assessment tasks, although they make greater cognitive demands than the other methods. Judgment tasks are particularly well suited for exploring semantic variation. Standardized tests are generally used to focus on syntax and vocabulary at the literal level of comprehension while the informal procedures in Chapter 4 can help in examining comprehension strategies and the all-important area of classroom comprehension. These procedures can be used to augment other types of assessment, to examine comprehension of higher-order language, and to look at classroom-based problems with comprehension.

James

James is an 8-year-old boy in the second grade whose production skills are characterized by an MLU that is higher than expected (+1 SD) for 8-year-olds. He displays a high number of repetitions and revisions and other forms of mazes (i.e., false starts and abandoned utterances) in his speech (52 utterances in a 100-utterance sample). His PPVT–R score is at age level, as is his *Test of Auditory Comprehension for Language–Revised (TACL–R)* (Carrow-Woolfolk, 1985) score. This suggests that basic literal comprehension is not a problem. If we examine the production data, however, concern emerges about James's knowledge of complex syntax. His MLU could be interpreted as a sign of better-than-average syntactic skills. When a high MLU is combined with a high number of mazes, the relationship between the two measures must be considered. An evaluation of James's language sample revealed the mazes occurred in the longer utterances. Frequently, several mazes occurred in these utterances, all of which were attempts at multipropositional (i.e., complex) utterances. Simple sentences rarely contained mazes. If we assume that mazes occur either because James could not find the word he wanted or had trouble formulating the syntactic structure, then production data suggest a problem with complex syntax. With this in mind, we might ask whether James understands the syntax of complex sentences. The following assessment plan was developed with this question in mind.

Assessment Plan

Administer Procedure 4.1 to focus on the complex syntax items. Then move on to Procedures 4.2, to assess comprehension of passive sentences, and 4.4, to assess comprehension of center-embedded relative clauses. Procedure 4.3 may be given as a check on discourse-level comprehension skills.

Results

James performed well on the discourse-level comprehension task (Procedure 4.3), but failed all of the items evaluating complex syntax. It is hard to know whether this is due to limited memory or processing span, or to syntactic difficulty. In either case, intervention focusing on speaking in simple sentences is a logical first step. This will reduce revisions that are disruptive to intelligibility. Once simple sentences are established, we can address development of complex syntax in both receptive and expressive modes. James's good discourse-level skills will give him an advantage in this effort, because he already has a sense that different forms are appropriate for different social contexts. We can start from there, using sets of simple sentences, asking to whom it would be appropriate to say such sentences (e.g., a young child). We could then combine the two sentences into a complex one, pointing out differences in form and similarities in meaning between the simple and complex utterances. More practice with sentence combining, using curricular material and classroom literature, and focusing on using pragmatic contexts to choose between simple and complex forms could follow (see Paul [1995] for detailed procedures). When comprehension of complex forms has been strengthened, James might be encouraged to produce his own complex sentences by combining sentences or paraphrasing textbook material to include complex sentences. Word processing activities, or "talking" computer programs, can be used to vary these activities.

CHILDREN WITH SEVERE SPEECH IMPAIRMENTS

Assessing comprehension in children with severe motor or cognitive impairments presents significant challenges. In most cases, comprehension status is critical to understanding the child's language skill, because speech limitations make assessment of production extremely difficult. When evaluating an individual to determine the need for an augmentative or alternative communication (AAC) system, knowing about comprehension skills is especially important. Generally, the child's comprehension status will determine the type of symbols (concrete versus abstract) and the initial vocabulary set used. For children already using AAC devices, knowing comprehension status will help us to determine appropriate production targets, whether single symbol or symbol combinations. Finally, knowing when a child begins to comprehend some symbolic language can indicate readiness to move away from an iconic AAC system (e.g., a picture board) to a more symbolic one. For all of these reasons comprehension assessment is a central part of our mission in evaluating children with severe speech production impairments (SSPI).

Several tests have provided adaptations for persons with physical and cognitive impairments; these include the *Sequenced Inventory of Communication Development (SICD)* (Hedrick, Prather, & Tobin, 1975), the *Reynell Developmental Language Scales* (Reynell, 1985), and the *Non-speech Test* (Huer, 1983). In addition, many of the procedures in this volume can be adapted for use with children with SSPI.

Our first task in adapting any procedure is to identify, usually by trial and error, some reliable response the child can make. This might include activating a switch by suck/puff or a small motor movement (e.g., pointing with a headstick, indicating a general direction with a hand movement, gazing at an object to indicate an "eye-point" response). Another method to try is "dependent auditory scanning." Here a child with limited pointing or eye-pointing skills can be given a sentence (e.g., "The girl has a dog") and asked to indicate the picture that represents it by having the clinician point to it and ask "Is it this one?" The clinician does this for each picture in the array until the child indicates a "yes" response with whatever movement is available. Once a reliable method of responding has been established, we can use it to have the child indicate a choice among two or four pictures, as a yes/no answer, or to indicate a judgment.

As with any child, the type of response we can expect will depend on general developmental level. If developmental level has not already been established, we can get an approximation by adapting a cognitive assessment. The *Raven's Coloured and Standard Progressive Matrices* (Raven, 1965) is especially helpful because it uses a pointing response. The choices can be placed on a child's communication board and he or she can indicate an answer by whatever response mode has been established. For children with developmental levels below 5 years, picture-pointing and yes/no responses are most appropriate. Judgment tasks, like those in Chapter 4, can be used with children whose nonverbal abilities are above the preschool level. The two most commonly used tasks for children with SSPI are eye pointing and yes/no judgments.

Eye Pointing to Pictures or Objects

Looking as a response for comprehension and recognition tasks has been used successfully for children as young as several weeks of age. It is used in testing infants' visual acuity (*Teller Visual Acuity Cards* [1989]), and has also been incorporated into the *Reynell Developmental Language Scales* (Reynell, 1985) adaptation for persons with physical impairments. Eye pointing is a powerful tool, but to use it successfully, we must be sure the individual being tested has adequate control of vision. This seems obvious, but we often assume visual competency without confirmation, something no clinician would assume about hearing. Any standardized picture comprehension test or any procedure in this volume using pictures can be adapted to an eye-pointing task. For example, in Procedure 3.7, simply copy the picture plates and cut them apart. Place the pictures at equal distances with enough separation to ensure identification of a distinct look. Distance and angle will vary for each individual. The clinician's ability to recognize a distinct looking response will determine the arrangement. Begin using the corners of a wheelchair lap tray, moving the pictures closer together as necessary. The further apart the pictures are placed, the more time the child will need for scanning. Pictures can also be placed on an elevated plastic frame to provide the most direct visual angle, or we can ask the child to look toward the corner of the room that corresponds to the choice. This exaggerated response instruction provides a bigger target that is easily interpreted. If the child cannot eye point in all four directions, the dependent auditory scanning technique discussed earlier can be used. Remember: Developing the testing arrangement is a trial-and-error process. It may take a number of sessions to complete testing because of fatigue. Make a game of it, and remember that comprehension abilities of persons with severe impairments are usually estimations. This is not an exact science. Any reliable information about comprehension will help develop effective interventions for facilitating comprehension of verbal messages, as well as improved message production for children with SSPI.

Yes/No Judgment Tasks

Judgment tasks are ideal methods for testing the comprehension of a variety of forms and functions because they require minimal responding. Any way to indicate yes or no, first or second, or right or left will do. Eye blinks, switches, or expanded keyboards, for example, can be used, so long as cognitive level exceeds the preschool range. The method of indicating should be individualized. Follow the suggestions for adapting picture-pointing tasks in placing the choices for judgment procedures. Dependent auditory scanning, as discussed previously, can also be used. Procedure 4.4 provides one example of a yes/no response strategy. Try using this response method for the stimuli from the procedures in earlier chapters or items that you develop. The major task in evaluating comprehension in these populations is developing a consistent response system. Take your time. The payoff in information gathered and clinical implications drawn will be well worth the effort.

Max

Max is a 16-year-old boy who was struck by a truck while skateboarding. Because he was not wearing a helmet, he experienced severe head injury and was in a coma for 24 hours. When he awoke, he appeared responsive but did not speak. After 2 weeks in a rehabilitation hospital, he continued to show increases in his awareness of his surroundings, but still made no vocalizations. He seemed frustrated, too, with his inability to communicate.

Assessment Plan

An assessment was undertaken to determine if an AAC system could help Max, even if it were only a temporary expedient until some vocal skills were recovered. The first question to answer was what response could be elicited. After several trials, it was found that Max's hand movements were not reliable enough to indicate a choice, but he could use a headstick to point to pictures displayed on a wheelchair table. This response proved reliable, and Max was willing to proceed with more testing. His clinician first needed to learn how much intellectual ability Max retained, in order to decide whether a symbolic system (e.g., writing) or a simpler, more iconic system (e.g., a picturebook) would be most helpful to him. Items from the *Raven's Coloured and Standard Progressive Matrices* (Raven, 1965) were copied, enlarged, cut apart, and mounted on his wheelchair table. Max was able to complete this test, although he was quite fatigued toward the end. The next day his literal comprehension was assessed, using the *TACL–R* (Carrow-Woolfolk, 1985), again copying and cutting up the pictures so he could indicate a choice with a head-stick. To get an idea of his discourse-level comprehension, Procedure 4.3 was given. Max was able to indicate a yes/no response by raising his eyes for yes and closing them to indicate no. Reading skill was also assessed, using the *Peabody Individual Achievement (PIAT) Reading Recognition Test* (Dunn & Markwardt, 1981) and having Max point with his headstick to the written version of the word pronounced by the examiner.

Results

Max scored at an 8-year level on the *Raven's Coloured and Standard Progressive Matrices* (Raven, 1965), a decrement from his performance before the accident, but a level that would allow him to use a symbolic form of communication. His literal comprehension was at a similar level. However, he had trouble judging the appropriateness of speech in context on Procedure 4.3. Max was able to recognize many printed words, scoring at least at a third-grade level on the *PIAT*.

Because Max's literal comprehension and reading recognition were adequate, it was decided to introduce a letterboard with which he could spell out messages with his headstick. This greatly reduced Max's frustration, but he still had problems with pragmatic aspects of language, as his discourse comprehension assessment results indicated. As Max's recovery continued, work on improving his expressive communication was supplemented with attention to pragmatic and discourse-level aspects of his comprehension and production.

References

Bangs, T.E. (1976). *Vocabulary Comprehension Scale (VCS)*. Austin, TX: Learning Concepts.

Barrett, M., Zachman, L., & Huisingh, R. (1988). *Assessing Semantic Skills Through Everyday Themes (ASSET)*. East Moline, IL: LinguiSystems.

Bellugi-Klima, U. (1968). *Evaluating the child's language competence* (Unpublished Report No. ED-019-141). Washington, DC: National Laboratory on Early Childhood Education.

Bishop, D. (1982). *Test for the Reception of Grammar (TROG)*. Unpublished test.

Bishop, D., & Edmundson, A. (1987). Language-impaired 4-year-olds: Distinguishing transient from persistent impairment. *Journal of Speech and Hearing, 52*, 156–173.

Bloom, L., Rocissano, L., & Hood, L. (1976). Adult–child discourse: Developmental interaction between information processing and linguistic knowledge. *Cognitive Psychology, 8*, 521–552.

Boehm, A.E. (1971). *Boehm Test of Basic Concepts–Preschool*. San Antonio, TX: Psychological Corporation.

Bracken, B. (1984). *Bracken Basic Concept Scale (BBCS)*. San Antonio, TX: Psychological Corporation.

Brinton, B., & Fujiki, M. (1989). *Conversational management with language-impaired children*. Rockville, MD: Aspen.

Bzoch, K., & League, R. (1971). *Receptive-Expressive Emergent Language (REEL) Scale*. Austin, TX: PRO-ED.

Carrow-Woolfolk, E. (1985). *Test of Auditory Comprehension for Language–Revised (TACL–R)*. Allen, TX: DLM Teaching Resources.

Carrow-Woolfolk, E. (1988). *Theory, assessment and intervention in language disorders: An integrative approach*. Philadelphia: Grune & Stratton.

Chapman, R. (1973, November). *The development of question comprehension in preschool children*. Paper presented at the meeting of the American Speech-Language-Hearing Association, San Francisco.

Chapman, R. (1978). Comprehension strategies in children. In J.F. Kavanaugh & W. Strange (Eds.), *Language and speech in the laboratory, school, and clinic* (pp. 309–327). Cambridge, MA: MIT Press.

Chapman, R. (1981). Exploring children's communicative intents. In J. Miller (Ed.), *Assessing language production in children: Experimental procedures* (pp. 111–138). Baltimore: University Park Press.

Chapman, R. (1992). *Processes in language acquisition and disorders*. St. Louis, MO: C.V. Mosby.

Chapman, R., & Miller, J. (1975). Word order in early two and three word utterances: Does production precede comprehension? *Journal of Speech and Hearing Research, 18*, 355–371.

Chapman, R., & Miller, J. (1983). Early stages of comprehension and discourse: Implications for language intervention. In R. Golinkoff (Ed.), *The transition from prelinguistic to linguistic communication: Issues and implications* (pp. 219–233). New York: Academic Press.

Chapman, R.S., & Miller, J.F. (1980). Analyzing language and communication in the child. In R.L. Schiefelbusch (Ed.), *Nonspeech language and communication* (pp. 159–196). Baltimore: University Park Press.

de Villiers, J., & de Villiers, P. (1973). Development of the use of word order in comprehension. *Journal of Psycholinguistic Research, 2*(4), 331–341.

Dickinson, D., Wolf, M., & Stotsky, S. (1993). Words move: The interwoven development of oral and written language. In J. Gleason (Ed.), *The development of language* (3rd ed., pp. 369–420). New York: Charles E. Merrill.

DiSimoni, F. (1978). *Token Test for Children*. Chicago: Riverside Publishing.

Dunn, L., & Dunn, L. (1981). *Peabody Picture Vocabulary Test–Revised (PPVT–R)*. Circle Pines, MN: American Guidance Service.

Dunn, L., & Markwardt, F. (1981). *Peabody Individual Achievement Test (PIAT)*. Circle Pines, MN: American Guidance Service.

Dunst, C. (1981). *A clinical and educational manual for use with the Uzgiris and Hunt Scales of Infant Psychological Development*. Baltimore: University Park Press.

Edmonston, N.K., & Thane, N.L. (1993). *Test of Relational Concepts*. Austin, TX: PRO-ED.

Engen, E., & Engen, T. (1983). *Rhode Island Test of Language Structure (RITLS)*. Austin, TX: PRO-ED.

Fenson, L., Dale, P., Reznick, J.S., Thal, D., Bates, E., Hartung, J., Pethick, S., & Reilly, J. (1993). *MacArthur Communicative Development Inventories (CDI)*. San Diego, CA: Singular Publishing Group.

Fey, M. (1986). *Language intervention with young children*. Needham, MA: Allyn & Bacon.

Gardner, M. (1985). *Receptive One-Word Picture Vocabulary Test (ROWPVT)*. Austin, TX: PRO-ED.

Graham, N.C. (1974). *Test of Preschool Language Proficiency*. Goster Green, Birmingham, England: University of Aston, Birmingham.

Greenfield, P. (1978). Informativeness, presupposition, and semantic choice in single-word utterances. In N. Waterson & C. Snow (Eds.), *The development of communication* (pp. 443–452). New York: John Wiley & Sons.

Hammill, D. (1992). *Detroit Tests of Learning Aptitude–III*. Austin, TX: PRO-ED.

Hammill, D.D., & Bryant, B.R. (1991). *Detroit Test of Learning Aptitude–Primary 2 (DTLA–P)*. Chicago: Riverside Publishing.

Haynes, W., & Shulman, B. (1994). *Communication development: Foundations, processes, and clinical applications*. Englewood Cliffs, NJ: Prentice Hall.

Hedrick, D.L., Prather, E.M., & Tobin, A.R. (1975). *Sequenced Inventory of Communication Development (SICD)*. Seattle: University of Washington Press.

Hodun, A. (1975). *Comprehension and the development of spatial and temporal sequence terms*. Unpublished doctoral dissertation, University of Wisconsin–Madison.

Hresko, W.P., Reid, K., & Hammill, D.D. (1991). *Test of Early Language Development (TELD–2)*. Austin, TX: PRO-ED.

Huer, M. (1983). *Non-speech Test*. Wawkonda, IL: Don Johnston Developmental Equipment, Inc.

Irwin, J.V., Norris, W.M., Deen, C.C., Greis, A.B., Cooley, V., Auwenshine, A., & Taylor, F.C. (1973a). *Lexington Developmental Scale (LDS)*. Lexington, KY: United Cerebral Palsy of Bluegrass.

Irwin, J.V., Norris, W.M., Deen, C.C., Greis, A.B., Cooley, V., Auwenshine, A., & Taylor, F.C. (1973b). *Lexington Developmental Scale Screening Instrument (LDSSI)*. Lexington, KY: United Cerebral Palsy of Bluegrass.

James, S., & Miller, J. (1973). Children's awareness of semantic constraints in sentences. *Child Development, 44*, 69–76.

Lahey, M. (1988). *Language disorders and language development*. New York: Macmillan.

Lahey, M. (1990). Who shall be called language disordered? Some reflections and one perspective. *Journal of Speech and Hearing Disorders, 55*, 612–620.

Lee, L. (1971). *Northwestern Syntax Screening Test (NSST)*. Evanston, IL: Northwestern University Press.

Miller, J. (1978). Assessing children's language behavior: A developmental process approach. In R.L. Schiefelbusch (Ed.), *The basis of language intervention* (pp. 269–318). Baltimore: University Park Press.

Miller, J. (1981). *Assessing language production in children: Experimental procedures*. Baltimore: University Park Press.

Miller, J. (1988). The developmental asynchrony of language development in children with Down syndrome. In L. Nadal (Ed.), *The psychobiology of Down syndrome* (pp. 167–198). New York: Academic Press.

Miller, J. (1992). Lexical acquisition in children with Down syndrome. In R.S. Chapman (Ed.), *Child talk: Advances in language acquisition* (pp. 202–216). Chicago: Yearbook Medical Publishers.

Miller, J., Campbell, T., Chapman, R., & Weismer, S. (1984). Language behavior in acquired childhood aphasia. In A. Holland (Ed.), *Recent advances: Language disorders in children* (pp. 57–99). San Diego: College-Hill Press.

Miller, J., & Chapman, R. (1981). The relation between age and mean length of utterance in morphemes. *Journal of Speech and Hearing Research, 24*, 151–161.

Miller, J., & Leadholm, B. (1992). *Language sample analysis guide: The Wisconsin guide for the identification and description of language impairment in children*. Madison: Wisconsin Department of Public Instruction.

Miller, J., & Yoder, D. (1984). *The Miller–Yoder (M–Y) Test of Grammatical Comprehension.* Baltimore: University Park Press.

Miller, J.F. (1987a). A grammatical characterization of language disorder. *Proceedings of the First International Symposium in Specific Speech and Language Disorders in Children* (pp. 100–113). London, England: Association for All Speech Impaired Children.

Miller, J.F. (1987b). Language and communication characteristics of children with Down syndrome. In S.M. Pueschel, C. Tingey, J.E. Rynders, A.C. Crocker, & D.M. Crutcher (Eds.), *New perspectives on Down syndrome* (pp. 233–262). Baltimore: Paul H. Brookes Publishing Co.

Miller, J.F., Chapman, R.S., Branston, M., & Reichle, J. (1980). Language comprehension in sensorimotor stages V and VI. *Journal of Speech and Hearing Research, 23*(2), 284–311.

Miller, J.F., Leavitt, L.A., & Leddy, M. (in press). *Communication development in young children with Down syndrome.* Baltimore: Paul H. Brookes Publishing Co.

Nelson, N. (1992). *Childhood language disorders in context: Infancy through adolescence.* New York: Charles E. Merrill.

Newcomer, P., & Hammill, D. (1988). *Test of Language Development–2 Primary (TOLD–2).* Austin, TX: PRO-ED.

Owens, R. (1992). *Language development: An introduction* (3rd ed.). New York: Charles E. Merrill.

Paul, R. (1981). Assessing complex sentences. In J. Miller, *Assessing language production in children: Experimental procedures* (pp. 36–40). Baltimore: University Park Press.

Paul, R. (1985). The emergence of pragmatic comprehension: A study of children's understanding of sentence-structure cues to given/new information. *Journal of Child Language, 12*(1), 161–180.

Paul, R. (1990). Comprehension strategies: World knowledge and the development of sentence comprehension. *Topics in Language Disorders, 10,* 45–62.

Paul, R. (1993). Patterns of development in late talkers: Preschool years. *Journal of Childhood Communication Disorders, 15,* 7–14.

Paul, R. (1995). *Child language disorders from birth through adolescence: Assessment and intervention.* St. Louis, MO: C.V. Mosby.

Paul, R., & Shiffer, M. (1991). Communicative initiations in normal and late-talking toddlers. *Applied Psycholinguistics, 12,* 419–432.

Porch, B.E. (1974). *Porch Index of Communicative Ability in Children (PICA–Children).* Palo Alto, CA: Consulting Psychologists Press.

Raven, J. (1965). *Raven's Coloured and Standard Progressive Matrices.* San Antonio, TX: Psychological Corporation.

Rees, N., & Shulman, B. (1978). I don't understand what you mean by comprehension. *Journal of Speech and Hearing Disorders, 43*(2), 208–219.

Rescorla, L. (1989). The Language Development Survey: A screening tool for delayed language toddlers. *Journal of Speech and Hearing Disorders, 54,* 587–599.

Reynell, J. (1985). *Reynell Developmental Language Scales.* Los Angeles: Webster Psychological Services.

Richard, G., & Hanner, M.A. (1985). *Language Processing Test (LPT).* East Moline, IL: LinguiSystems.

Shatz, M., & Gelman, R. (1973). The development of communication skills: Modifications in the speech of young children as a function of listener. *Monograph of the Society for Research in Child Development, 38.*

Sparrow, S., Balla, D., & Cicchetti, D. (1984). *Vineland Adaptive Behavior Scales (VABS).* Circle Pines, MN: American Guidance Service.

Swift, E., & Rosin, P. (1990). A remediation sequence to improve speech intelligibility for students with Down syndrome. *Language, Speech, and Hearing in the School, 21,* 140–146.

Teller Visual Acuity Cards. (1989). (Available from Stereo Optical Co., 3539 North Kenton Avenue, Chicago, IL 60641–3879)

Vygotsky, L. (1962). *Thought and language.* Cambridge, MA: MIT Press.

Westby, C. (1991). Learning to talk—talking to learn: Oral-literate language differences. In C. Simon (Ed.), *Communication skills and classroom success: Therapy methodologies for language-learning disabled students* (pp. 181–218). San Diego: College-Hill Press.

Wetherby, A., Cain, D., Yonclas, D., & Walker, V. (1988). Analysis of intentional communication of normal children from the prelinguistic to the multiword stage. *Journal of Speech and Hearing Research, 31,* 240–252.

Wetherby, A., & Prizant, B. (1989). The expression of communicative intent: Assessment guidelines. *Seminars in Speech and Language, 10,* 77–91.

Wetherby, A., & Prizant, B. (1990). *Communication and Symbolic Behavior Scales.* Chicago: Riverside Publishers.

Wetherby, A., & Prutting, C. (1984). Profiles of communicative and cognitive-social abilities in autistic children. *Journal of Speech and Hearing Research, 27,* 364–377.

Wiig, E.H., Second, W., & Semel, E. (1992). *Clinical Evaluation of Language Fundamentals–Preschool (CELF–Preschool).* San Antonio, TX: Psychological Corporation.

Woodcock, R.W. (1991). *Woodcock Language Proficiency Battery–Revised.* Chicago: Riverside Publishing.

Zimmerman, I., Steiner, V., & Pond, R. (1992). *Preschool Language Scale–3 (PLS–3).* San Antonio, TX: Psychological Corporation.

Glossary

Behavioral compliance   Any observable response by an individual viewed in terms of stimulus, response, or consequence that meets the task criteria of the examiner.

Brown's stages   The stages during which 1.0–4.5 morphemes occur in an average sentence produced by a child. This range typically corresponds to 2–5 years of age.

Complex sentence   A sentence containing a main clause and one or more subordinate clauses; includes more than one main verb.

Conjoined sentence   A sentence that is composed of two independent clauses joined by a linking word or a conjunction.

Contextualized   Occurring in the immediate environment of the speaker and listener, including past experiences that each brings to the situation.

Contingent (response type)   Dependent on, and related to, a stimulus utterance.

Contrived   Unlike the communication styles and patterns that appear in ordinary day-to-day communication.

Criterion-referenced test   Assessment of an individual's development of certain skills in terms of absolute levels of mastery. Performance is not compared to that of peers, but only to the predetermined mastery criteria.

Decontextualized   Language with little information outside of the linguistic signal itself to help a listener derive meaning.

Extralinguistic cues   Additional information that accompanies the linguistic signal and helps the listener understand what is being said. Examples include intonation, gestures, facial expression, and objects and events in the environment.

Illocutionary force   The speaker's intent in a communication act; that which a speaker is performing when verbalizing (e.g., thanking, promising, requesting, describing, reporting).

Imitative (response type)   Response that copies, almost exactly, an utterance spoken previously by a conversational partner; a direct repetition of a previous speaker's utterance.

Locative prepositions   Prepositions that pertain to location or spatial orientation of the state or action named by the verb (e.g., *in, on, under, beside*).

Mean length of utterance (MLU)   Average length of oral expressions as measured by a representative sampling of oral language, usually obtained by counting the number of morphemes per utterance and dividing by the number of utterances.

Metalinguistic ability   Ability to think about language and to comment on it, as well as to produce and comprehend it; language awareness—a temporary shift in attention from what is being said to the language used to say it; ability to reflect on language.

Morphological markers   Specific endings attached to words, such as the *ing* ending on verbs or the possessive *'s* attached to nouns.

Naturalistic   Similar to communication styles and patterns that appear in ordinary day-to-day communication.

Noncontingent (response type)   An utterance not dependent or semantically related to the utterance that precedes it.

Norm-referenced scores   Scores designed to compare an individual's performance to that of individuals in a norming sample. Tests that yield standard or age-equivalent scores are norm-referenced.

Normative   Referring to information that is measured against a set of norms; compares a given score to scores received by a large group of individuals tested under standardized conditions.

Object permanence   Awareness that an object is relatively permanent and is not destroyed if removed from the visual field (e.g., an individual is still present even if his face is covered by his hands).

Presuppositional skills   Ability to infer information that is not contained in the sentence but must be known and understood if that sentence is to make sense; the ability to use shared knowledge and information given by the context to augment understanding of a language.

Psychometric   Psychological and mental testing.

Receptive language   Understanding of linguistic communication; may be visual or spoken; spoken or written messages received by the individual.

Reliability   The dependability of a test as reflected in the consistency of its scores upon repeated measurements of the same group; the stability of the score; the degree to which a score is free of random error.

Simple sentence   Sentence containing one main clause, one main verb, and no subordinate clauses.

Standard error of measurement   A derived score that uses as its unit the standard deviation of the population upon which the test was standardized. The standard error of measurement is used to determine a confidence interval around a subject's score. The confidence interval represents the range of scores within which a client's ideal "true" score is likely to fall, given the score the client actually obtained on any particular administration of the test.

Standardized test   Test administered to a group of students to determine uniform or standard procedures and methods of interpretation.

Validity   Extent to which a test measures that which it is intended to measure; the degree to which a test is free of bias, or systematic error.

Index

Page numbers followed by "f" indicate figures; those followed by "t" indicate tables